BRICK
VEHICLES

BRICK VEHICLES

AMAZING AIR, LAND, AND SEA MACHINES TO BUILD FROM LEGO®

WARREN ELSMORE

BARRON'S

A Quintet Book

First edition for the United States and Canada
published in 2015 by Barron's Educational Series, Inc.

All inquiries should be addressed to:
Barron's Educational Series, Inc.
250 Wireless Boulevard
Hauppauge, NY 11788
www.barronseduc.com

Library of Congress Control Number: 2014930731
ISBN 978-1-4380-0530-0
QTT.BHW

This book was conceived, designed, and produced by
Quintet Publishing Limited
114–116 Western Road
Hove, East Sussex
BN3 1DD
United Kingdom

Photographer: Michael Wolchover (unless otherwise stated)
Designer: Gareth Butterworth
Art Director: Michael Charles
Project Editor: Caroline Elliker
Editorial Assistants: Ella Lines, Alice Sambrook
Editorial Director: Emma Bastow
Publisher: Mark Searle

10 9 8 7 6 5 4 3 2

Printed in China by Toppan Leefung

CONTENTS

INTRODUCTION

ON THE ROAD

OFF THE RAILS

MAKING WAVES

TAKING FLIGHT

WELCOME TO BRICK VEHICLES!

It's been said that the first thing humans invented was the wheel, so what better topic to choose for a look at transport throughout the ages?

Brick Vehicles is the fourth in my LEGO® series, after *Brick City*, *Brick Wonders*, and *Brick Flicks*. In this book we take a journey through time and space, looking at how men and women have been transported around the planet. Each topic that we cover is recreated in LEGO bricks, and many of these models have a full set of instructions so you can build them at home!

Creating models of planes, trains, and automobiles is a popular topic for LEGO fans of all ages and has been since bricks were invented. So for *Brick Vehicles,* rather than "reinventing the wheel," I've chosen to feature some of my favorite builders and their amazing creations. I've included models from LEGO fans everywhere, from Europe to Australia, as a way to say "thank you" to these builders.

Our first chapter looks at transport on the road—cars, trucks, and much more. We start with the Roman chariots that covered the empire hundreds of years ago. Mechanized transport is introduced with the Penny Farthing—the earliest bicycle—before we take a look at the vehicles on the road today. Motorcycles and sidecars pass by as the truck delivers your LEGO sets and the snow plow clears the track!

The second chapter explores some really heavy haulage. We take a look at the rails and investigate trains of all types. Besides historic and modern locomotives, we also include other rail-driven vehicles. One of these is the monorail that you may have seen on your vacations, and we even include instructions to build your own minifigure roller coaster cars!

Leaving terra firma behind, in our third chapter we take to the waves with all manner of seafaring

devices. We have traditional trawlers searching for fish and container ships covering the oceans, as well as more historic vessels. The huge hovercraft ferries that were built to connect England to France, as well as the earliest "ironclad" warships are included, and if you want a little light relief, how about building some water skis?

The final chapter of *Brick Vehicles* takes to the skies and beyond. We look at planes, balloons, blimps, gliders, parachutes, and even space transport! After conquering land and sea, the obvious way to travel is in the air. Whether you are traveling on a famous commercial airliner such as the Concorde, in the luxury of a private jet, or even on one of the first commercial space flights, this has to be the best way to travel!

Although I've tried to cover a wide range of vehicles in *Brick Vehicles*, the list is a long one and there are so many different types of transport that we've just not been able to fit all of them in. But don't let that worry you, because one thing is certain—LEGO® sets with wheels are always on sale, so there is no shortage of wheels available for your own creations! What type of brick vehicle will you build for your minifigs? A car? A train? A boat? A plane? Or maybe even something completely new and different. With LEGO bricks, the sky is the limit!

— Warren Elsmore

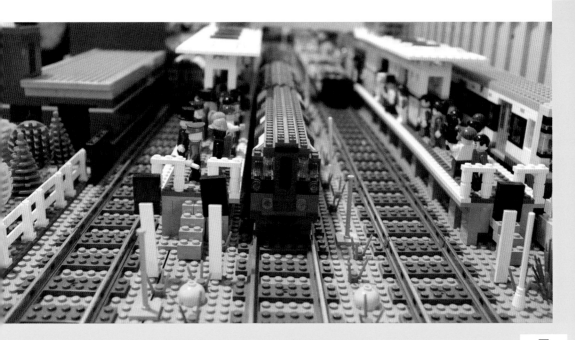

NAMING BRICKS

This is a 2 x 4 brick, but perhaps it's a 4 x 2 brick? Or an "eight-er" or even a "Rory?" Did you know that all LEGO® elements have official names? If you're buying parts to build some of the models in the book, it will probably help to know what these names are.

There are two main naming schemes for LEGO elements. The first, of course, is from The LEGO Group, which obviously has a name for each brick it produces.

The second naming scheme is used by the adult fans of LEGO within LDraw and BrickLink.

The LEGO naming scheme is fairly straightforward—with a few exceptions. The basic unit is of course a brick—like this 1 x 1 brick on the left.

From there, the naming references the short side first. So these are 1 x 1, 1 x 2, 1 x 3, and 1 x 4 bricks:

Of course, you might call the longer brick a "four-er." But then, how would you distinguish between these bricks? They all have four studs.

This is why most LEGO fans will use the same naming, so it's easier to ask our friends if they have any 2 × 2 round bricks or 1 × 4 bricks. A common naming convention means that we're both looking for the same part. Of course, once your bricks are organized, it's time to move onto "plates," "tiles," and "slopes." The same naming structure applies, and now you have the four basic types of elements that LEGO produces.

Of course, there are many other types of elements produced, many of which are highly specialized and look nothing like a brick. So, in general, I use the term "elements" to refer to LEGO parts, whatever the shape, especially when special bricks are involved. This, for instance, is a 1 × 1 Brick with One Knob.

As The LEGO® Group is a Danish company, the word "knob" is the English translation of a Danish word. This is also where the fan naming tends to diverge from LEGO's own names—partly because of the influence of American fans and the English language on the Internet. In English, at least, the protruding part of the brick is called a "stud" rather than a "knob." Of course, that varies by country as well—the Dutch would call it a "nop" and the Danish, "knop." Matters become even more complicated when you're dealing with arch bricks.

So, which name is "correct?" Well, whereas the LEGO name might be the official name, that's not to say that any other name is wrong. The brick on the left, for instance, is a 1 x 2 Palisade Brick.

But ask any fan for a Palisade Brick, and they won't know what you are talking about. To fans, this is a 1 x 2 Log Brick, and this is where the problems lie. The chances are that you, like me, will order bricks from LEGO and also from BrickLink, or buy them from other fans. So, sadly, there's no easy way around it. In some cases, you just need to know both names, especially with bricks like this one to the right, which is both Brick 2 x 1 x 1⅓ with Curved Top AND Brick W. Arch 1 x 1 x 1⅓.

1 x 4 Arch Brick OR Brick with Bow 1 x 4
and 1 x 4 Curved Slope OR… Brick with Bow 1 x 4

WHERE TO BUY LEGO®

The most common question that I've been asked since the release of *Brick City* is "where do you buy your LEGO from?" The simple answer is "the same places you do," but of course when building models as large as I do, the real answer is more complicated.

A common misconception is that The LEGO Group doesn't sell boxes of "just bricks" anymore. This isn't true. In fact, a fellow U.K.-based AFOL (Adult Fan of LEGO) did some research on this and published his findings online: http://bigsalsbrickblog.blogspot.co.uk/2014/08/it-was-all-basic-bricks-in-my-day-part.html. His research shows that I can still buy the bricks I used as a kid today!

So where do I buy my bricks? Well, firstly I buy a lot of LEGO sets—especially if I'm after certain pieces. Some of my models need pieces that aren't easy to find, and if there is a set on the shelves that has that piece, then I will buy the whole set for just that piece!

Mainly, though, I use online stores that sell LEGO parts. The two most well known are brickowl.com and bricklink.com. These stores both work like eBay, but they specialize in LEGO. The stores have catalogs of almost all the LEGO elements ever produced and show which independent sellers have them for sale. It can take some time to find all the pieces, but you can be assured that when the parts turn up, you'll have exactly what you need.

If I'm building a large model, however, I tend to work around the available bricks from the place where I can buy most of them. For me, that's the local LEGO Brand Retail Store (the big stores in the malls with "LEGO" above the door). These stores and LEGOLAND parks both have what is known as a "Pick A Brick" wall. Here, you can fill a container with as many bricks as you can fit into it—for a fixed price. The real advantage of "Pick A Brick" is that the LEGO elements are available in large quantities. Take

the runway of my airport, for instance. That uses an estimated 10,000 2 x 2 light gray tiles. That's a lot of tiles for anyone to own, but when the parts became available in my local store, I jumped on them! In fact, that's why the runway is light gray instead of, for instance, dark gray. That color choice alone probably saved me hundreds of pounds!

If you're too far from a LEGO store, or the parts you're after aren't available at your store (the selection is limited), then there is one last avenue—the online LEGO Shop (http://shop.lego.com/en-US/). The LEGO website has an online "Pick A Brick" section with a much larger selection of pieces. It's more expensive per piece than visiting a local store, but you might just be able to get the piece that you need!

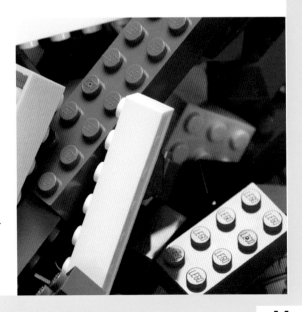

CAD Modeling

No matter how many LEGO® bricks you might own, you'll certainly never have enough! So how do you build your favorite model without having all of the right bricks at hand? When designing the models for *Brick Vehicles*, I used LEGO CAD software.

CAD (Computer-Aided Design) software lets you play with virtual LEGO bricks to create an amazing model. With an unlimited number of bricks at your disposal, in any color you like, there's nothing to stop you from creating the ultimate LEGO model. There are two main types of LEGO CAD systems available to use, and both are free!

LEGO Digital Designer (ldd.lego.com) is available for free download from LEGO and is available for Mac or PC. Once you have installed the software it will download a list of all the (currently) available LEGO bricks for you to build with. Expect this to take some time as there are a lot of bricks to choose between!

The newer versions of LEGO Digital Designer now include a standard mode or an "Extended Mode." While the standard mode will only allow you to use

bricks in colors that exist, "Extended Mode" doesn't have such a restriction, letting you build your models from a huge range of bricks.

One of the real benefits of LDD is that it's designed to help you build a creation that will work in the real world—so bricks will be automatically connected for you as you place them. Once finished, LDD can even create online instructions for you so you can build the model in the real world. Just switch the model into "Building Guide Mode" and follow the steps.

The LDraw system (www.ldraw.org) is the second type of LEGO CAD system available. LDraw pre-dates LDD, and rather than being written by the LEGO Group, the LDraw system was created and is maintained by the LEGO community itself—fans like you and me.

So if LEGO produces free design software, why use anything else? Well, for me LDraw has a few significant advantages. Firstly, almost any part ever made is available in the LDraw system. That's a much larger list than is available in LDD, and sometimes an older

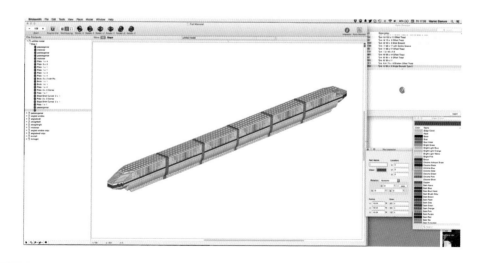

part works perfectly to recreate a feature in a certain model. Every single part has been painstakingly drawn based on the physical parts.

Secondly, editing software using the LDraw system is far more flexible than LEGO® Digital Designer. For instance, the tool I use—Bricksmith—will let you create models that wouldn't really work in the real world. When designing a model I sometimes just use a 1 x 1 brick for everything—to layout the overall shape. Of course, if I tried to do that in real life, the model would just fall apart. Modeling on the computer, though, that's not something I need to worry about—it's much faster to not have to worry about how a model might actually stay together.

When building a larger creation, it's also handy to be able to do things that wouldn't work in real life while I fine tune a model. The ability to place two bricks in the same physical space means that I can slide bricks along without worrying about the studs. It's also a very easy task to replace two 1 x 4 bricks with a 1 x 8 brick without being concerned about the bricks above or below it.

There is a downside to all this flexibility of course. Using the LDraw system you will have to work out for yourself how to build that model so it will hold together and create your own instructions. The benefits outweigh these disadvantages for me though, and I've used LDraw for all the models in this book.

The LDraw system supports a wide range of different tools that you can use to create models and instructions. Although each tool works slightly differently, they do all use the same core library of parts. For this book, I have used the Bricksmith editor on the Mac to create the models and the LPub tool to create their instructions. I am extremely grateful to all those involved for their hard work in creating this software, and to everyone involved at LDraw.org.

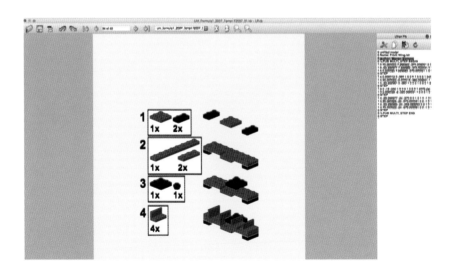

PRACTICE PROJECT

SOAPBOX RACE CAR

Brick vehicles come in many shapes and sizes, so what's the best way to start your own brick vehicles project? Let's start where so many young Americans have begun their racing or mechanic careers—a Soapbox Derby!

Soapbox racing wasn't something I did when I grew up, but I'm sure I would have jumped at it given the chance! The challenge is simple—create the fastest downhill race kart that is powered by gravity alone. There's no engine allowed—just creativity and a hill. The name, by the way, comes from the original boxes used to make the carts. Soap is not allowed!

One of the great things about soapbox racing is the variety of designs that can be made. Many are sleek and aerodynamic, but many are just for fun and can be totally wacky! So for our practice project, I've designed a very simple chassis that you can add your own soapbox design to.

The parts for this chassis are very easy to get, so you shouldn't have much trouble creating one of your own. The wheels, red plate, steering wheel, and seat are all common pieces, and the color you use doesn't matter.

I've used the 2 x 2 tile with one stud on the front and back so that different nose cones and tail pieces can be added and removed. If you don't have these though, don't worry—just build directly onto the red plate.

I've included some pictures of racers that we designed here in my studio, but I can't wait to see what you come up with!

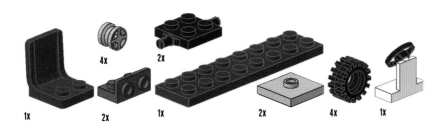

4x   2x

1x   2x   1x   2x   4x   1x

1

2

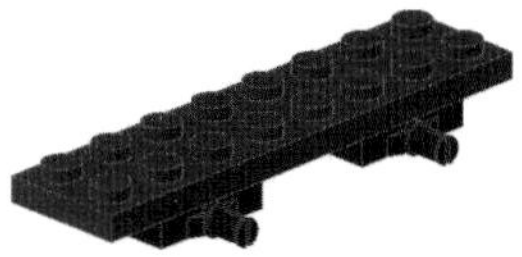

3

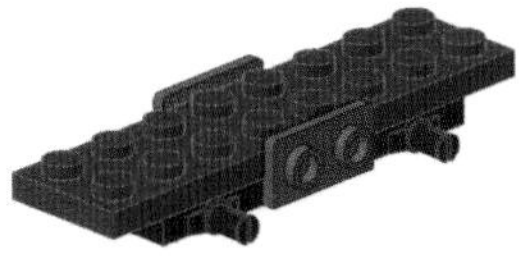

4

5

6

7

THE HISTORY OF THE LEGO® WHEEL

Did you know that the LEGO wheel is older than the LEGO brick itself? Much older, in fact!

The Danish founder of The LEGO Group, Ole Kirk Christiansen, started producing toys in the early 1930s. He ran a successful carpentry business building houses, but the economy wasn't doing too well at that point so he turned to toys instead.

We don't know what the first-ever toy produced was, but a quick look at the 1932 price list, in its original Danish, shows a few items that certainly had wheels: "Sportsbil" (Sports Car), "Lokomotiv" (Train), and "Legevogn" (Handcart). Wooden toy production continued for some time, with a variety of cars and pull-along toys being produced.

Wooden toys such as cars and trucks continued to be produced until they were slowly replaced by metal die-cast versions. In fact, it wasn't until the LEGO company started producing plastic toys that these wooden wheels finally stopped moving!

The LEGO brick, as we know it today, was patented at 1:58 p.m. on January 28, 1958. With the birth of the LEGO brick, there were a number of sets produced—and even spare part packs as well—so it was possible to build houses and garages quite easily. What didn't exist, though, was a LEGO wheel that could be attached to your bricks. At this time, if you had cars in your LEGO town, they would have been made of metal.

The introduction of the modern LEGO® wheel came in 1959—first in one set, then later in a whole range of sets. They were red, had LEGO studs on the sides, and had a metal axle pointing out the back. It was a particularly painful brick to step on!

This type of LEGO wheel continued to be produced for quite some time. Train varieties were produced (to fit onto rails), motorized versions were created (with a rough outside surface), and many other types were made. The size of these wheels varied as well—some had only one stud on the side, some four studs, and the largest had 12 studs. Eventually, though, these wheels were also replaced.

In the 1980s, the majority of the metal axle wheels were slowly replaced by plastic axles and then by LEGO plates that had axles built into them. Rather than having to replace the whole plate to change a wheel color, it was now possible to just change a car's wheels and tires—just like the real thing! The smallest axle connectors introduced in the 1980s are still around today, connecting wheels of all colors to a variety of tires and a massive range of vehicles.

Metal axles for LEGO wheels continue to be made, though. The demands of LEGO trains mean that a smooth-running wheel is essential, and metal is still needed to keep those trains running. Changing a wheel on a train, though, is a more complicated procedure!

Reflecting the vision of the founders of The LEGO Company, almost every LEGO wheel can now be connected in numerous ways. Whether you use a small axle or larger wheels that connect with LEGO Technic pins or axles, how you connect them together—and what you build—is completely up to you!

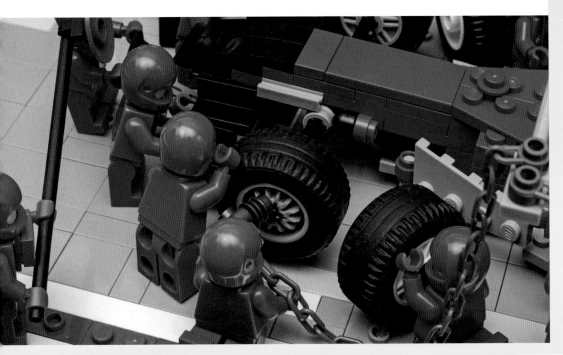

THE SCIENCE OF LEGO®

Have you ever wondered what makes LEGO bricks so special? The way they can easily be pulled apart when you want to build something new, but how strong they can be when you need them to be? There is a lot of science that goes into making a LEGO brick, and I've been lucky enough to talk to lots of people who work for The LEGO Group to find out more.

That strength you can feel when clicking together bricks is what LEGO calls "clutch." When designing construction bricks, it's important to make sure that they stay together once the model has been built. Making sure that the bricks have enough "clutch power" is essential in keeping your model together, but too much clutch power and you won't be able to pull the bricks apart!

The LEGO Group has carefully measured just how much clutch power is required for your models to

stay together, and every brick that's produced has the right amount of grip on each LEGO stud to hold together. If you also have LEGO Duplo in the house, try seeing how well those bricks connect. Duplo bricks are designed for younger hands, which have less gripping power, so the clutch is that little bit weaker.

The colors of LEGO bricks are also very important to the LEGO company. If I am building a model in red, then sometimes I want all the bricks to be the same color—the same red. If you have other construction toys in the house, take a look at their bricks. Are they all the same color?

Keeping colors consistent isn't too difficult if all the bricks are the same, but LEGO produces thousands of different parts. What you might not know is that all LEGO bricks are not produced from the same material! Most LEGO bricks are made from a plastic

called ABS, but some other complicated or flexible parts are made from other materials. This means that the LEGO® company is constantly monitoring the parts that it produces to make sure that different parts—made in different materials—are in the exact same colors.

Have you ever wondered what it might take to squash a LEGO brick? If you built a huge model, would the bricks at the bottom start to sag? Well, the Materials Stress Lab of The Open University in the United Kingdom put this to the test.

The university tested a single 2 x 2 brick, which is a fair representation of most bricks, and used an industrial machine to measure how much pressure they could put on it until something happened. The result was that after loading up the brick with 770 lbs (350 kg) of weight, it slowly gave way and squashed flat! To put that in perspective, this amount of weight is equivalent to a tower of bricks 2.17 miles (3.5 km) high. So your models are fairly safe. For now…

The Open University experiment
Photography © David Phillips

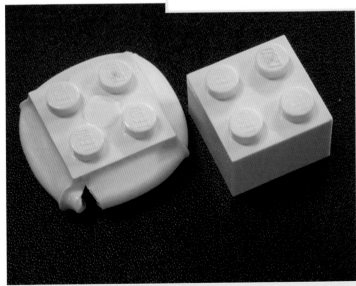

Gold Mine Evolution model by Tim Ross

These days LEGO® enthusiasts from all over the world are spoiled for choice when it comes to live events and exhibitions. They offer expert builders an opportunity to showcase their best work while giving LEGO fans of all ages an opportunity to marvel at the creations made possible with a bit of patience, hard work, and imagination. These photographs were taken at BRICK 2014, a live exhibition held at the ExCeL

Centre, London, supported by The LEGO Group. The fantastic four-day event, attended by nearly 50,000 people, was packed full of LEGO—and everything to do with it. There were hundreds of creations from the world's best LEGO builders, construction zones, great LEGO games, themed interactive areas, a huge store selling LEGO sets, and literally millions of bricks to play with—every LEGO enthusiast's dream!

Model by Bert Giesen

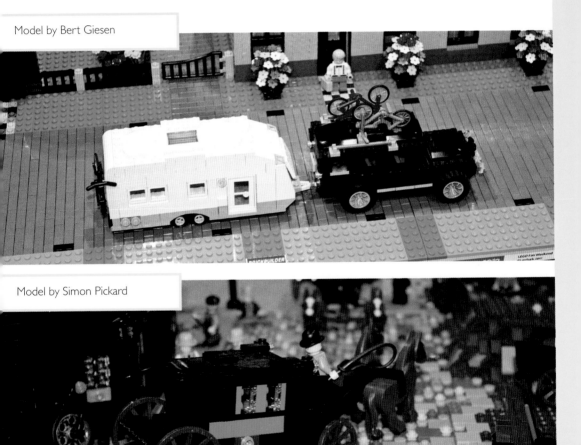

Model by Simon Pickard

Mosaics

LEGO® mosaics are, in principle, very straightforward. There are a limited number of LEGO colors, but more than enough to create a good picture. So the difficulties you may encounter will be related to the choice of image and how to best bring that out in LEGO tiles. Here are a few tips to help along the way.

Choosing your mosaic picture is the first challenge. You may be creating a mosaic of yourself, your favorite cartoon character, or any other image you like. To create a mosaic with maximum impact, try to stay away from images that are particularly complex. The more shades or fine detail an image has, the harder it will be to convert it into a recognizable LEGO mosaic—at least without making it absolutely enormous! So if you can, stick to a simple image with bold colors and features. I'm going to assume from here that you have this image on your computer.

There are many ways of converting your image into a LEGO mosaic. Really, a LEGO mosaic is just a low-resolution version of the image. You can try reducing the definition of the picture on your computer until it starts to become pixelated, as though it's made from LEGO tiles. However, this doesn't always work: You will often find that the image becomes unrecognizable, or that there are too many colors in it. This is where LEGO mosaic software comes in handy.

There are lots of software programs that will let you turn your image into a LEGO mosaic by reducing the colors and size automatically. I've used Pictobrick (www.pictobrick.de) and Photobricks (www.photobricksapp.com) for the mosaics in this book. Both are fairly simple to use, and will ask you how large you'd like the mosaic and what method to use to cut down the number of colors. Once finished, you'll get an output of what bricks go where, and you then just copy the image down in LEGO.

Anything is possible with a LEGO mosaic. World records are toppling all the time, with mosaics regularly being built from more than a million bricks. So if you have the desire to build it, it can be done!

Mosaics from *Brick Wonders*. Aurora Australis (below) and Internet cables (right).

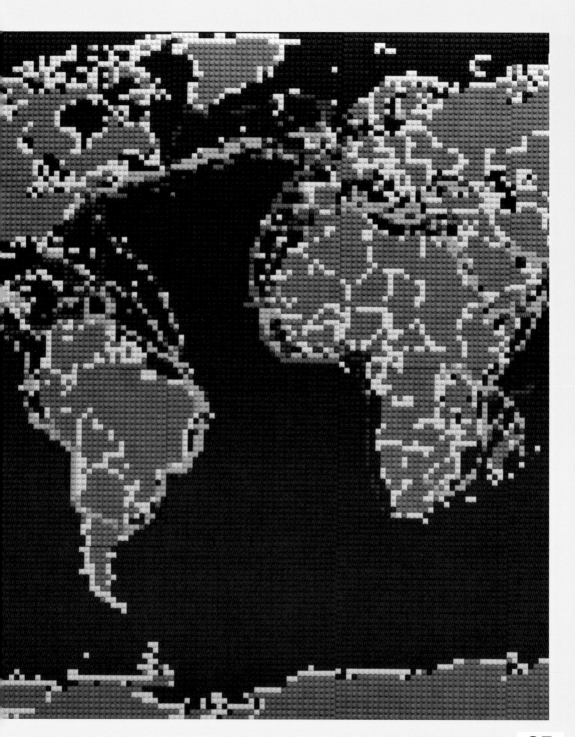

MINIFIGS

Minifigures were first created in 1978 and there are now nearly 4 billion in existence, with keen collectors located across the globe. Minifigs often come with LEGO® sets and are now also sold alone or as keychains or magnets. There are also many licensed film character minifigs such as those shown below, made by U.K.-based customizers Minifigs.me.

No LEGO scene is complete without minifigures to complement it, and Minifigs.me supplies most of our customized LEGO minifigures. Each one is made with extreme care and attention to detail. If they can capture tiny details such as facial expression, the figure comes to life with a charm all of its own. They can work for hours perfecting the costume, but it's the little human quirks that give a figure its soul.

After Minifigs.me has received the design, it's a matter of carefully selecting just the right parts to do the minifig justice. Once they have the blank figure ready, they feed it into a super high-tech printer. Whether it's a film star or a bespoke minifig for a customer, the final result is something very special.

STOP MOTION

Did you know that LEGO® lends itself well to stop-motion animation? There has been a huge interest in this kind of animation in recent years, resulting in many music videos and films being uploaded on social media sites, often attracting millions of viewers. This was also helped by the release of *The LEGO Movie* in 2014. Glasgow-based teenager Morgan Spence is passionate about stop-motion films and made one using the models and minifigures in my previous LEGO book, *Brick Flicks*. His film has attracted over a million YouTube views! Growing up, Morgan's favorite things were LEGO and cameras. So when he was 12 years old, it made perfect sense to try and combine the two and bring LEGO models to life. This led to his early adventures in stop-motion animation.

So, what is stop-motion animation? Well, it involves taking many still pictures and then playing them together at a high speed to create the illusion that the object you're animating is moving. The process can be time-consuming as the character, vehicle, or object to be animated will be moved a tiny amount for each photograph, with the process then repeated several hundred times to create a few seconds of moving footage. Morgan shoots his films at 15FPS, so 15 frames per second of film. The most famous recent example of stop-motion animation is probably Aardman Animations' *Wallace and Gromit*.

Morgan's first films were made using his dad's digital camera and free animation software that can easily be sourced from the Internet (iStopMotion: http://boinx.com/istopmotion/mac/ and Helium Frog: http://www.heliumfrog.com/ are two). With these simple tools and your LEGO creations (perhaps even some of the model ideas in this book!), you can achieve some pretty amazing results. My first efforts were all action and high drama: LEGO jail breaks, car chases, and train crashes! In 2013, Morgan was lucky enough to have one of his films chosen to support my *Brick City* touring exhibition. After this, Morgan made more films, bringing my fabulous *Brick Wonders* models to life and recreating famous Hollywood moments using the *Brick Flicks* characters. These can be viewed on his website: morgspennyproductions.co.uk.

Photography © Morgan Spence

27

When making stop-motion films, it helps to be organized ahead of shooting. After coming up with ideas, Morgan makes storyboards that map out the plot and thinks about different camera angles to shoot that will make the film look interesting. All his ideas will be noted on the storyboards. One of the fun parts is, of course, building the LEGO® sets and casting the minifigure characters. Whether it's a scene in a busy street or a modern office, he thinks about the small details he can add to make it look authentic. Finally, he is ready to film. He works in a darkened room (animation and natural light don't mix—imagine filming in a sunlit room and then the sun disappearing behind a cloud and changing the lighting of your entire shot). The set will be lit with lamps and other small lighting effects. The entire time Morgan's filming, he's also thinking about sound effects and the soundtrack, because these can make a big difference to the finished film.

Over time, Morgan has invested in a better camera and more professional animation and editing software—it all helps to make a good-looking film.

I should also mention patience—you will need a lot of it, especially at first! But, practice makes perfect! It is fun to do and well worth persevering—it's a great feeling to see your creations come to life on the screen. I urge you to give it a go—let your imagination run wild as you bring your brick vehicles to life!

Sorting and Storing

There is one perennial problem when it comes to LEGO® bricks—sorting them! Unless you have a very small collection, it soon becomes apparent that trying to find the right LEGO element can take more time than actually building the model. So, what to do? What is the best way of sorting your bricks?

If you do have a very small collection—perhaps only one or two sets—then the obvious way to sort your LEGO is to not sort it at all. With few bricks to choose between, storing all the bricks in one box is an appealing thought. Having said that, though, even if you do have a large amount of LEGO, there is a benefit to using this approach. Although I build in a studio, with huge numbers of bricks available in every color, sometimes my most creative builds come from using only a small number of parts. Or building from a mixed pile of LEGO—taking inspiration from those parts available and at hand. Not sorting your LEGO can actually help sometimes.

As your LEGO collection grows, however, most people will choose to sort their LEGO so it's easier to store and build from them. There are lots of ways to do this, but the most common methods chosen are either by color or by brick. Sorting by color is often the first way that LEGO fans decide to arrange their bricks. If you want to make a white house, then surely it's easier to build from a box of white bricks?

Sorting by color has one distinct disadvantage, though—black. Sorting through a box of black bricks is very difficult unless you have very bright lights. Black parts all seem to combine together so that you can never find the part you're looking for. As your collection grows, you'll also start to find that sorting by color becomes unmanageable. When you have a large box of blue, how can you find that one blue 1 x 2 brick with studs on both sides that you need?

Progressing from sorting by color, many fans then sort by type. Each different element has its own drawer or box, so it's easy to find a part. As your collection grows, however, you realize that perhaps every part having a drawer isn't so practical—you would need tens of thousands of drawers! So, elements are grouped together—all the LEGO Technic elements are stored together, perhaps, or all the tiles. Sorting by part works well for most medium-sized collections.

When you progress into "Master Builder" territory, or build professionally for a living like I do, then you need an approach that scales well. My studio contains many hundreds of thousands of bricks—almost certainly millions, although I've never counted. Professional builders mainly choose to sort by both part AND color. This means that it's easy to find one exact piece, but we can also quickly get hold of, for instance, all the gray bricks.

Each builder will have their own system that works the best for them. In fact, I actually have two systems running concurrently in my studio. Here's what I do.

When I'm planning a build, what's most important to me is the way that the bricks connect. So inside my office, the walls are surrounded by hundreds of small drawers—the same drawers that are used for storing screws. In these drawers, I keep elements by part, regardless of color. This means that if I want to check how one brick connects to another, I can quickly find the parts and check. Color isn't important to me here, as I'm usually prototyping a design to check if something will work correctly.

However, when I'm building a large model, such as the ones in *Brick Wonders*, it's important that I have the right shape and color of bricks. So this is where my main stores come into play. I store my bricks by part and by color. At the moment, my primary sort is by color, so I have a green section, a blue section, etc. Then within each section, I have a number of drawers, and within each drawer are the parts themselves. To make sure that the parts don't mix together, I store each part/color combination in a resealable bag.

So, if I'm building a small, quick model, I have everything at hand from my chair. If I'm building a large model, I can select the bags of parts that I need—or perhaps even remove entire drawers if I know I'll need, for instance, lots of white bricks.

There's only one real problem with having a well-sorted and stored LEGO® collection. You do, of course, have to sort the bricks first!

Online Resources

LEGO® fans of all ages have a huge and vibrant community, both in person and online. So if you've been inspired by my previous books, why not get involved yourself?

LEGO Message Boards

Most people's earliest interaction with other LEGO fans online is possibly through the LEGO Message Boards at community.LEGO.com. The LEGO Message Boards are the company's official forums run by The LEGO Group. The Message Boards are open to anyone who wants to take part, but because they are run by the official LEGO company, you'll need a LEGO ID to register and take part. The good news is that a LEGO ID is free to sign up for and very easy to get.

One important point to note about the LEGO Message Boards is that they are heavily moderated. There's no lower age limit on these forums, so to make sure that the content is safe for everyone, your posts are checked before they are made public. That doesn't mean there isn't a lively discussion and a large number of participants, though. As I write this, over 50,000 people are viewing the Message Boards.

ReBrick

ReBrick (at rebrick.LEGO.com) is the LEGO company's own social media platform. Aimed more at teenagers and adults than the LEGO Message Boards, ReBrick showcases the amazing array of creations that LEGO fans from around the world have made.

The idea behind ReBrick is not to store any pictures, videos, or links itself, but to provide LEGO fans with a way of bookmarking links to all that content in one place. If you've used Delicious, Pinterest, reddit, or Digg, then you'll find ReBrick very familiar. If you haven't used any of these sites, then think of ReBrick as a great resource of links to amazing LEGO content.

What you won't find on ReBrick are any official LEGO sets or sales pitches. Like much of the fan community, ReBrick concentrates on MOCs, or "My Own Creations"—models designed by LEGO fans like you and me.

LEGO CUUSOO

If you have ever wanted to create a LEGO set that you can see being sold in a shop, then LEGO CUUSOO (lego.cuusoo.com) is the site for you. CUUSOO is originally a Japanese idea, but is similar in ethos to the more widely known Kickstarter or Indiegogo. The sites' basic concept is that if an idea is well supported, then it can become a reality!

LEGO CUUSOO allows you to create your own original idea and submit it to the site. You don't need to have built the idea from LEGO, or even have a 100% finished idea, but you do need to have a great idea that will attract attention. Once you've submitted your idea to the CUUSOO site, it is then your task to promote that idea as widely as you can.

To turn an idea into a LEGO set, the first challenge is to rally 10,000 supporters to vote for your idea on the site. Then, four times a year, the CUUSOO team will review all of the projects that have reached the 10,000 mark to see which will be made into an official LEGO set. So far, four CUUSOO sets have been released, with many more projects already under consideration or in the production process. So, what are you waiting for?

Rebrickable

The LEGO® Group supports a wide range of websites, but once you step into the fan community, there is an even wider range of content available. Rebrickable (rebrickable.com) is a fan site that aims to solve the dilemma that all LEGO builders have at some point: Do I have enough bricks to build this?

Rebrickable allows you to browse a selection of individual creations with full lists of all the parts you'll need to build them. More than that, though, you can also upload a list of the official LEGO sets that you already own, and Rebrickable will tell you which models you can build with the bricks from those sets!

The Rebrickable site is a great example of a site that brings together multiple technologies developed by the LEGO fan community. By parsing the 3D CAD files created by LDraw editors and combining these with the information available at the online marketplace bricklink.com, the site creates a whole new way to decide what to build.

Blogs and Fan Sites

The list of LEGO blogs and fan sites grows longer every day. Some, like my own at warrenelsmore.com, are related to individual people. Others, like brickshelf.com, showcase creations from thousands of fans. There are news sites, discussion sites, and everything in between.

From the long list of websites, there are a few LEGO fan sites that I visit regularly that might prove a good place to start. Firstly, there's brickset.com, which bills itself as "the top online resource for LEGO collectors worldwide." Although I certainly wouldn't disagree with that statement—it's somewhat of an understatement! Brickset has the largest and most complete database of every LEGO set ever made, as well as the ability to record your own collection. The site also showcases the latest LEGO news and set reviews, as well as hosts a lively discussion forum.

Although based in Europe, eurobricks.com is certainly not confined to the continent. Eurobricks is based around a huge online discussion forum, but also highlights its members' creations and product news. Eurobricks is also well known for the set reviews created by its members. In fact, the standard of reviews is now so high that they have their own "academy" to teach new reviewers the ropes.

The final site that I frequent often is The Brothers Brick (www.brothers-brick.com). The Brothers Brick concentrates mainly on showcasing the best creations by LEGO fans from around the world. The general standard of models shown is very high and most builders are very happy to be featured on the site.

Flickr, YouTube, Facebook, et al...

Although there are a huge number of dedicated LEGO websites, online LEGO content isn't restricted to those. Whether your favorite online experience is Flickr, YouTube, Facebook, Twitter, or any other social media site, you can be guaranteed that LEGO fans will have a strong presence. Just search for "LEGO"!

ON THE ROAD

CABLE CAR

Although cable cars were installed in New York, Dunedin, Melbourne, and Sydney, it's in San Francisco that this cable car found its fame. Dragged along by a constantly moving cable underneath the city streets, the cars have a manually operated pickup underneath the car. To move forward, the operator simply "picks up" the cable and the vehicle is hauled along. To stop, it's simply "dropped." Sadly, cable cars never became popular as they proved too expensive to maintain. The tourists love them, though!

CABLE CAR

San Francisco's manually operated cable cars first ran in 1873, and three of the original lines are still in operation today. Routes are named after the streets on which they travel. Single-ended cars ride on Powell, Mason, and Hyde Streets and are rotated on turntables at each end, and double-ended cars run up and down California Street. Tourists can also enjoy the Cable Car Museum and an annual cable car bell-ringing competition, held every July in Union Square.

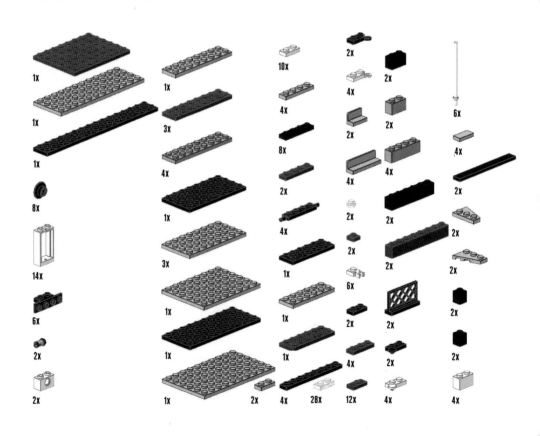

1

2

3

4

5

6

7

8

9

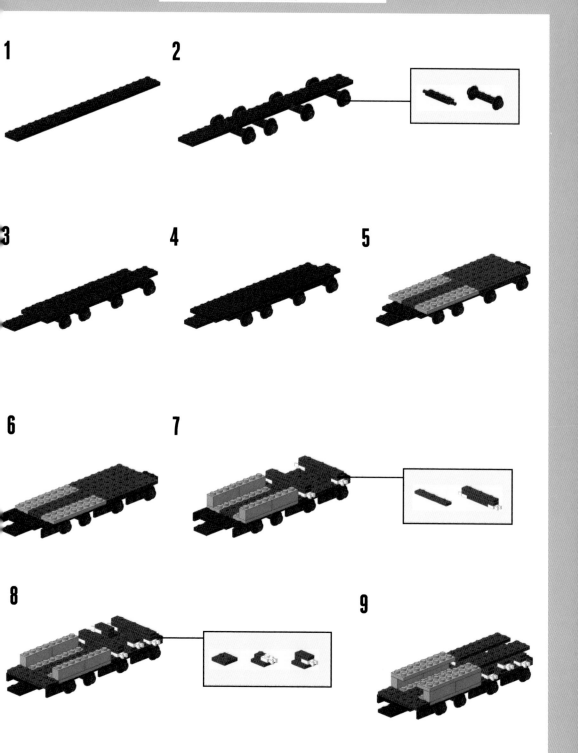

10

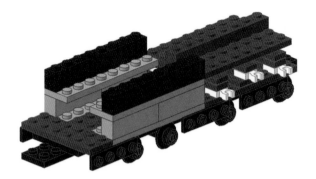

11

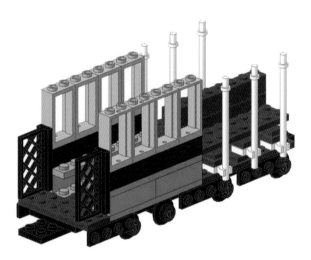

12

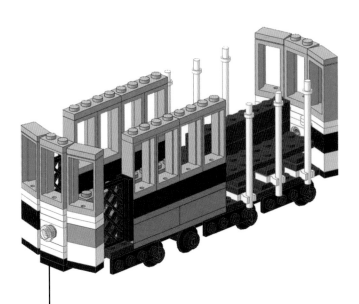

13

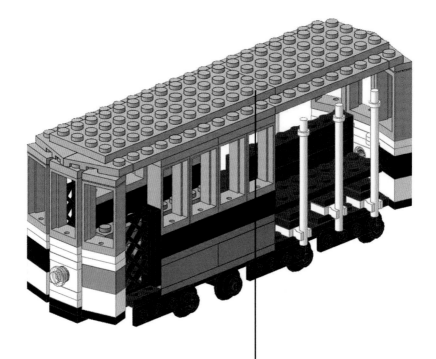

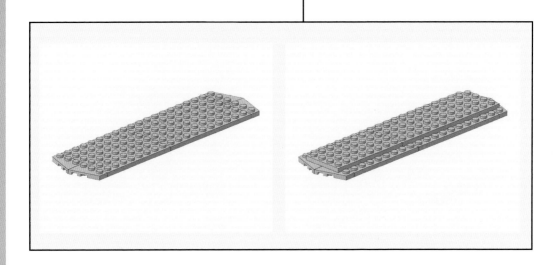

14

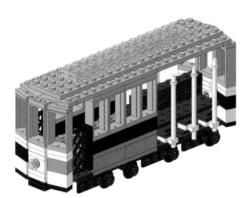

15

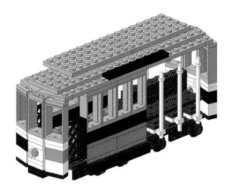

16

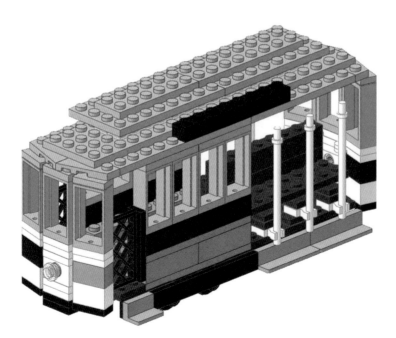

ROMAN CHARIOT

Chariots have been in use since at least 2,000 B.C. as a method of fast transport. Usually associated with waging war or racing, they are relatively simple devices consisting of an area to stand upon, a guard to protect the driver from the elements, and a hitching for one or more horses. Whereas their use in war had dwindled by the first century A.D., racing chariots remained popular for a long time—until at least the sixth century A.D.—and were immortalized in the 1959 film *Ben Hur*. This model is based on those used in the film.

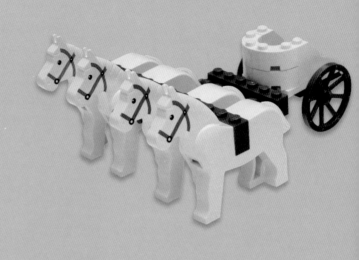

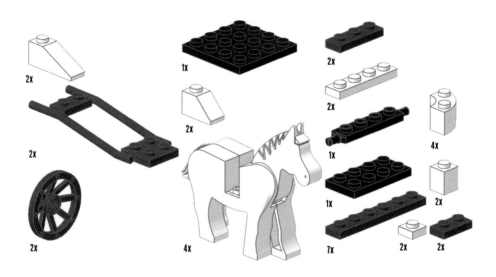

2x

1x

2x

2x

2x

2x

4x

2x

2x

1x

1x

2x

7x

2x

2x

4x

1 **2** **3**

4 **5**

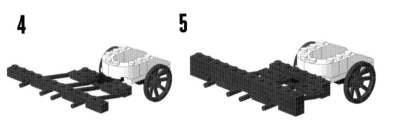

6

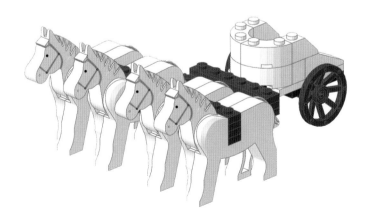

COMBINE HARVESTER

As some of the largest machines that can be found on a farm, combine harvesters are an essential part of any modern agriculture business. The name comes from the three tasks that the machine "combines"— reaping (cutting and gathering the crops), threshing (loosening the edible part of the grain), and winnowing (separating the grain from the chaff). Modern combine harvesters like this one are such large machines that it's common for them to have the front cutting head removed when the machines are moved between fields.

RICKSHAW

Rickshaws originated in Japan relatively recently—in the latter half of the 1800s. After a ban on wheeled vehicles was lifted, the rickshaw rapidly replaced the palanquin or "litter" (a covered chair carried by two or more people). Requiring only one person, the rickshaw was much more popular and soon became a common sight throughout Asia. These days, though, the rickshaw is not so common as they have almost all been replaced by "auto rickshaws"—with a manual cycle or motorcycle engine. At least that's easier on the operator!

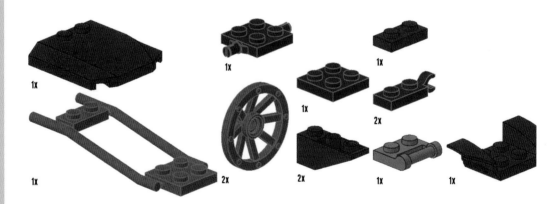

1x   1x   1x   1x   2x

1x   2x   2x   1x   1x

1

2

3

4

5

6

PENNY FARTHING BICYCLE
1870, Coventry, England

The "Penny Farthing" wasn't the first-ever bicycle made, but it's surely one of the most recognizable. The large front wheel gave the bicycle a good turn of speed on flat roads. Without any gears, the larger front wheel turned much further than that of the smaller "boneshaker" type that came before. The name "Penny Farthing" is taken from the sizes of the wheels, as they resemble two pre-decimal coins: the larger "Penny" and the smaller "Farthing" coins (a quarter of one cent), which were popular in Britain during the mid-nineteenth century. However, the bike was only christened after it went out of use. Victorians simply called it "a bicycle."

HORSE AND CARRIAGE

What better way to explore New York's Central Park, or be transported from your wedding to the reception? The horse and carriage is an ancient method of transport that is a popular novelty today. Whereas most journeys have now been replaced by cars, traveling in a horse-drawn carriage is still a romantic way to get around. This carriage is in white, as we imagine a LEGO® bride and groom ready to be picked up after their nuptials and taken to a reception for a party!

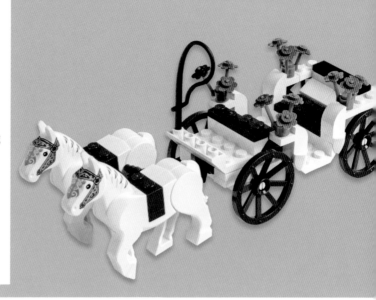

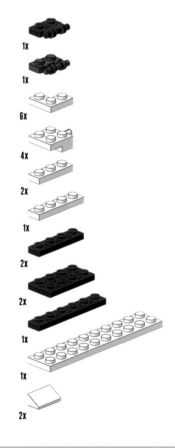

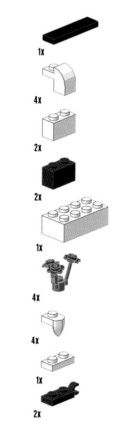

1

2

3

4

5

6

7

8

9

10

11

12

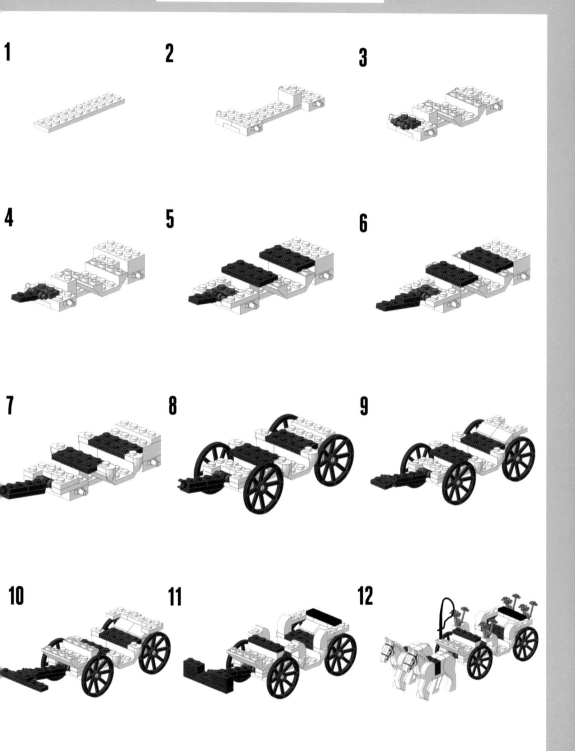

MOTORCYCLE SIDECAR

Motorcycle sidecars are almost as old as motorcycles themselves. In fact, they started out as bicycle sidecars! Sidecars have always been an easy way of moving two people with only one motor—in fact, the car company Jaguar originally started out as a manufacturer of motorcycle sidecars. The added stability of three wheels also helps move heavier items, and modern sidecars have been used by the armed forces, by medical agencies, and even as hearses.

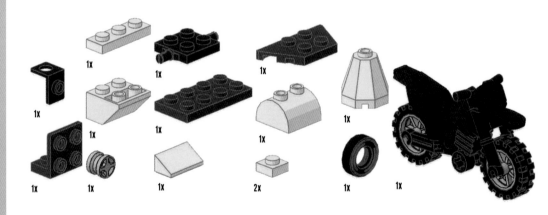

1x 1x 1x 1x 1x 1x

1x 1x 1x 2x 1x 1x

1

2

3

4

5

6

7

FORD MODEL T

1908, Detroit, U.S.A.

It's often said that Henry Ford deemed his cars could be "any color as long as it's black," but actually the original Model T was available in many different colors, and the cars have been painted almost every color since. Our LEGO® model is based on a 1927 model that still exists—on display at the Henry Ford Museum in Detroit.

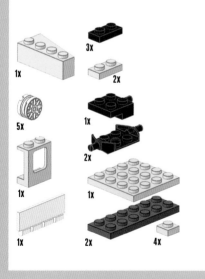

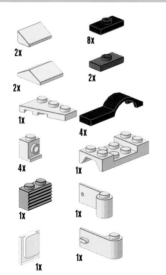

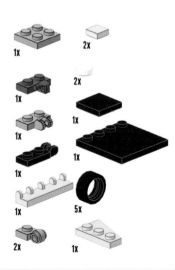

1

2

3

4

5

6

7

8

9

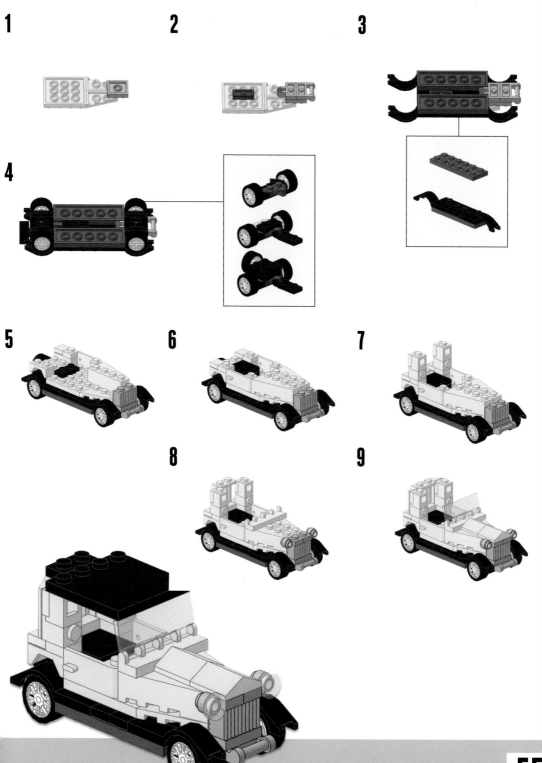

SNOW PLOW

The snow plow is a custom-designed truck with a large adjustable blade on the front to move snow from the road into the gutter. The large hopper on the back of the machine stores "grit"—or rock salt. Just don't drive your car too close to the snow plow—all that salt won't do your paintwork much good.

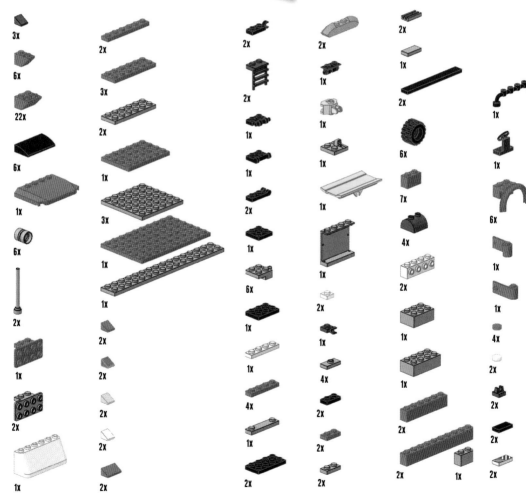

1

2

3

4

5

6

7

8

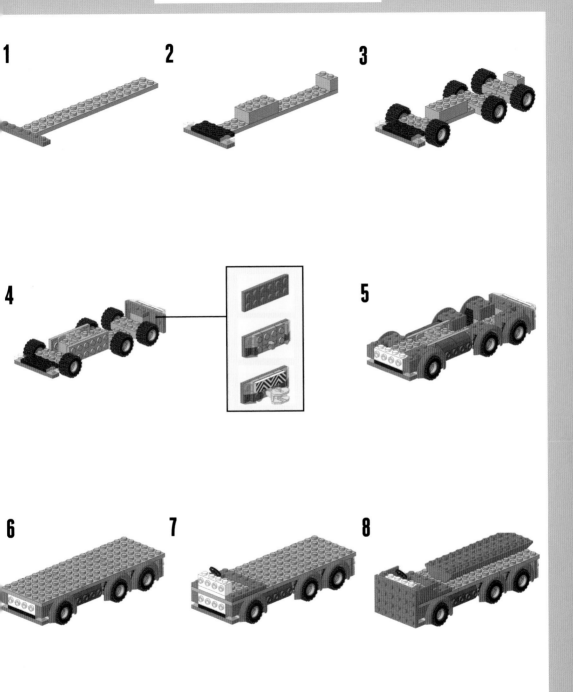

9

10

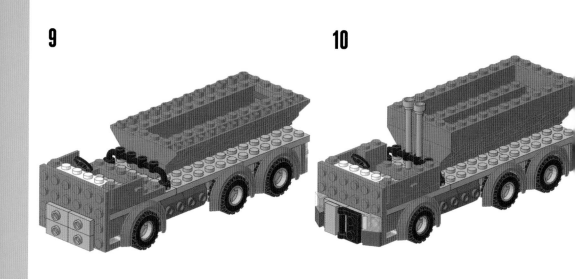

11

12

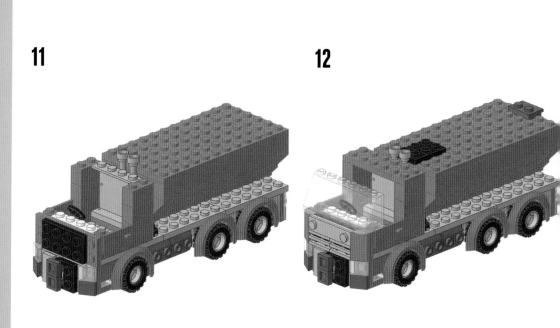

13

14

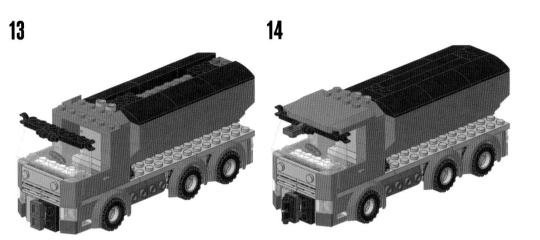

15

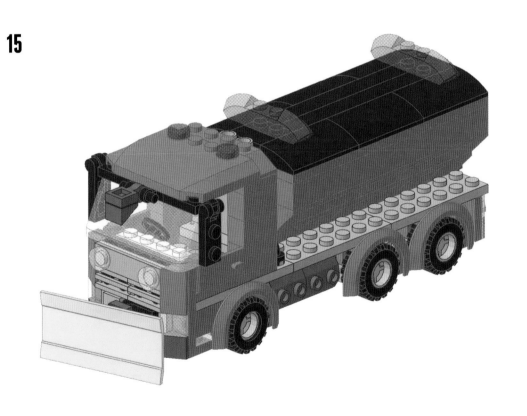

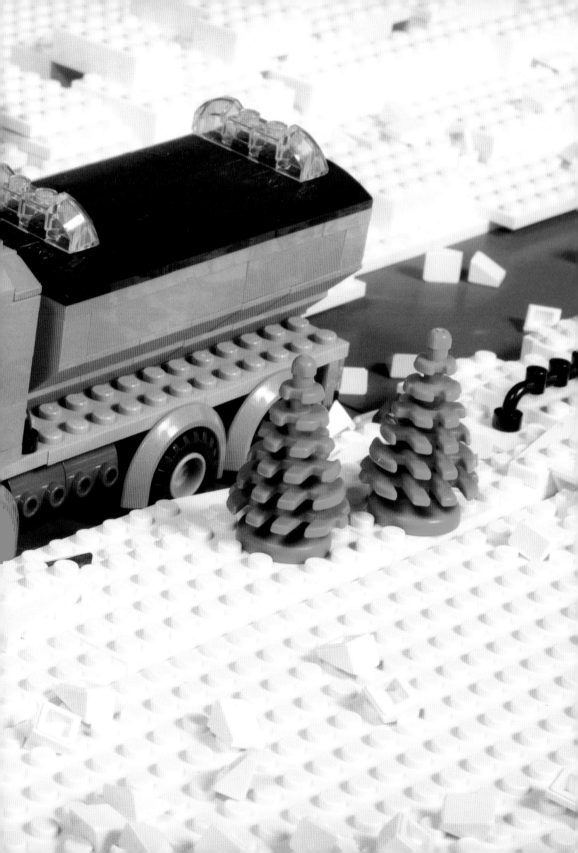

FIRE ENGINE

Fire engine trucks vary throughout the world, but this particular machine is based on one used in the United Kingdom. Not only must the truck carry fire fighters and water, it must also carry all the fire fighting equipment. In fact, although the vehicle may weigh many tons, it's unlikely that it will have more than 2 tons of water on board. Designed specifically with a large ladder on board, it enables fire fighters to reach the tops of tall buildings, or perhaps to just rescue a cat from a tree.

TRACTOR

Tractors are vehicles that are specifically designed to provide high torque at a low speed, or to put it more simply, "tractive power." Although they are very commonly seen on farms, tractors have become widely used in a variety of operations throughout the world. What's unique about farm tractors is the almost universal usage of the "three-point hitch." This clever mechanism allows different attachments to be quickly attached to and removed from the tractor.

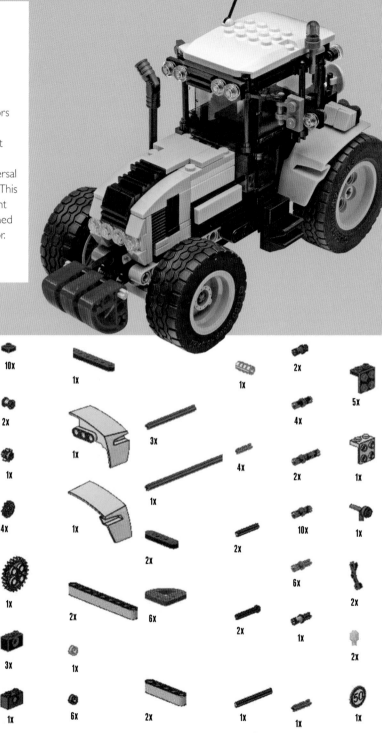

1x

1x

2x

2x

2x

2x

1x

1x

2x

2x

1x

10x

2x

1x

4x

2x

4x

1x

3x

1x

1x

2x

2x

2x

6x

6x

1x

1x

3x

2x

4x

1x

4x

2x

2x

2x

2x

1x

2x

10x

6x

1x

2x

1x

1x

5x

1x

1x

1x

2x

2x

1x

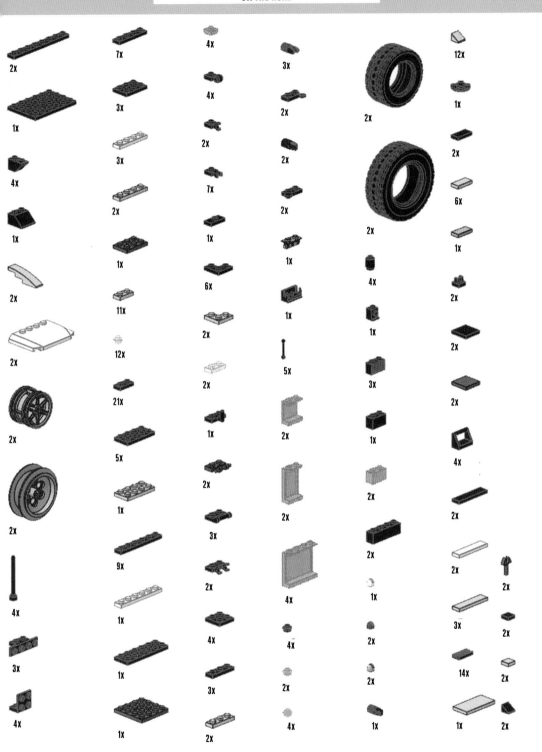

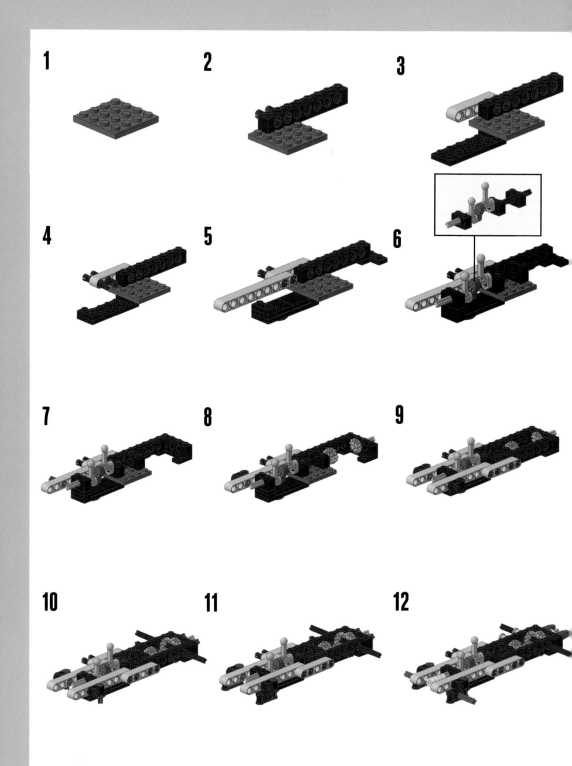

13

14

15

16

17

18

19

20

21

22

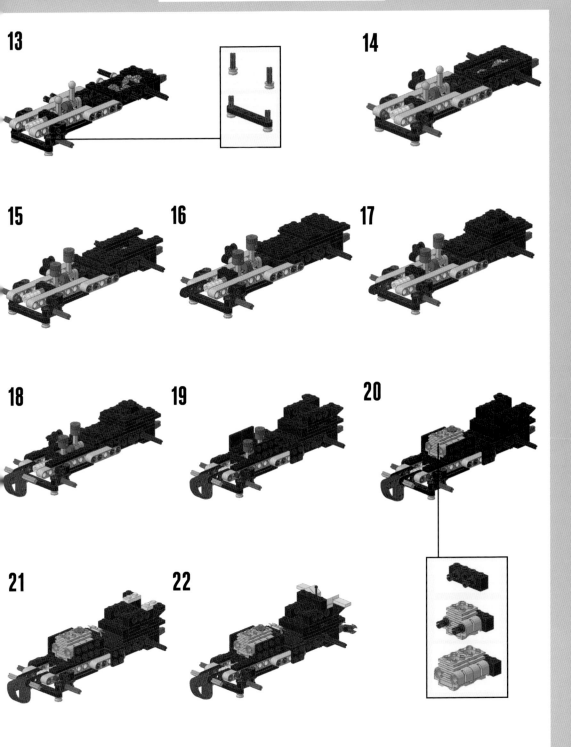

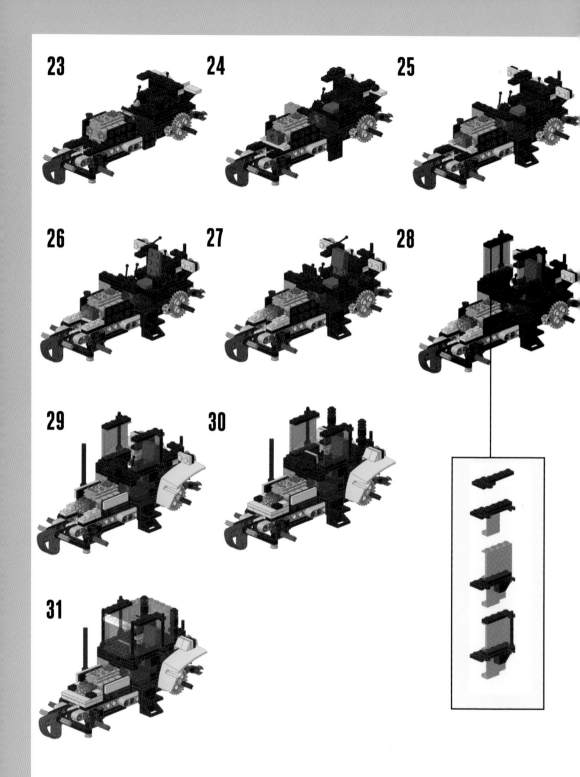

32

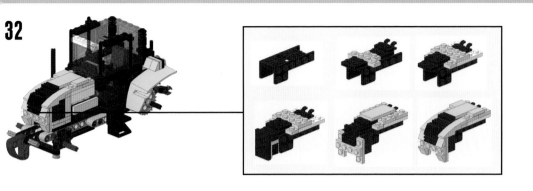

33

34

35

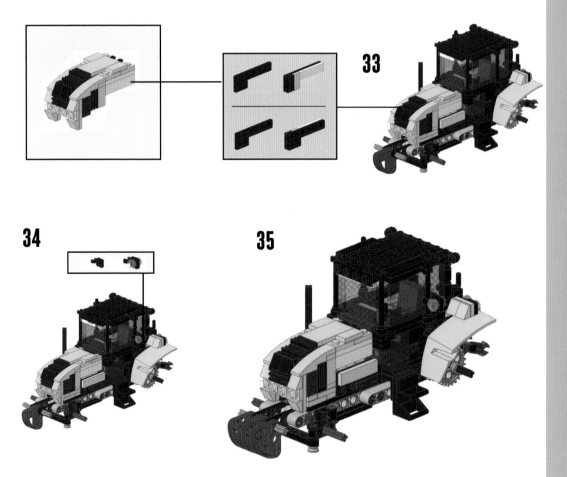

36

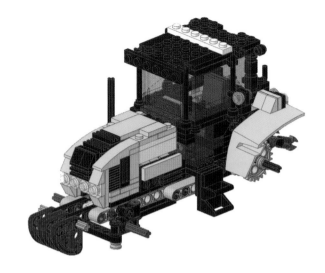

37

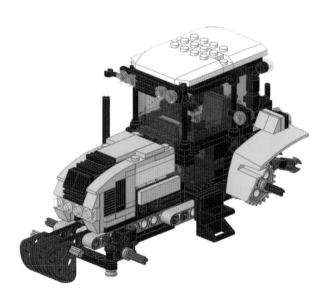

38

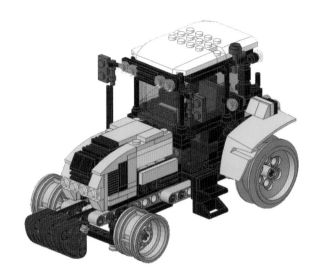

39

DOUBLE-DECKER BUS

1954, London, England

If you think of the shape of a
bus, it won't be long before this
shape comes to mind. This is the
famous London double-decker
bus. Built specifically for London,
it came into use in the late 1950s.
Featuring cutting-edge technology,
the bus was one of the first to use
a weight-saving aluminum body, as
well as provide power steering and
a fully automatic gearbox. Although
more than 60 years old now, many
are still operational in London and
around the world, proving that a
good design lasts.

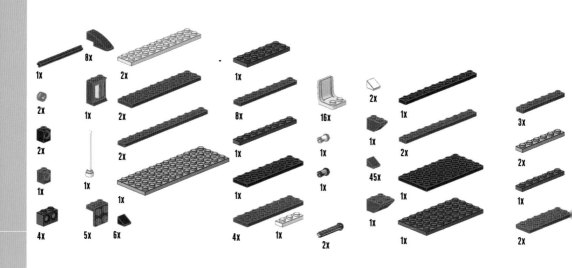

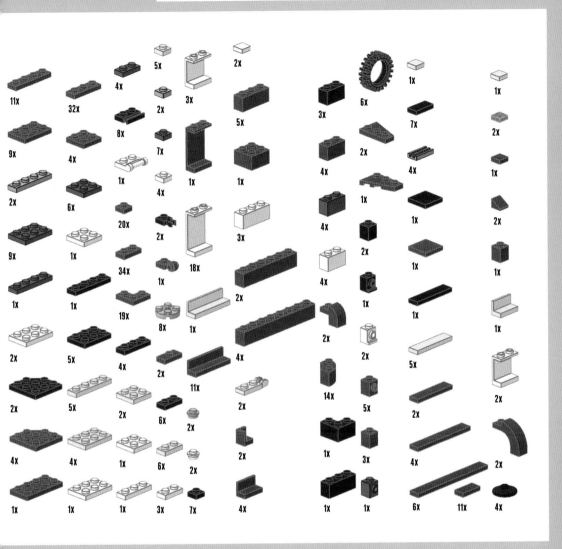

11x 32x 4x 5x 2x 6x 1x 1x

9x 4x 8x 3x 2x 5x 3x 7x 2x

2x 6x 1x 7x 2x 5x 2x 4x 1x

9x 1x 4x 1x 1x 4x 1x 1x 2x

1x 1x 20x 2x 3x 4x 2x 1x 1x

2x 5x 34x 18x 2x 4x 1x 1x

2x 5x 4x 8x 1x 4x 2x 2x 5x 1x

2x 5x 2x 11x 2x 14x 5x 2x 2x

4x 4x 1x 6x 2x 2x 1x 3x 4x 2x

1x 1x 1x 3x 7x 4x 1x 1x 6x 11x 4x

1　　　2　　　3

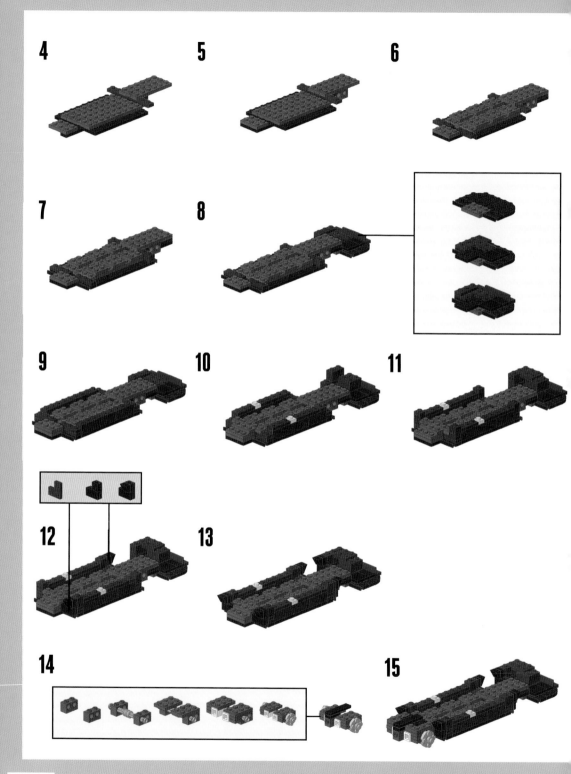

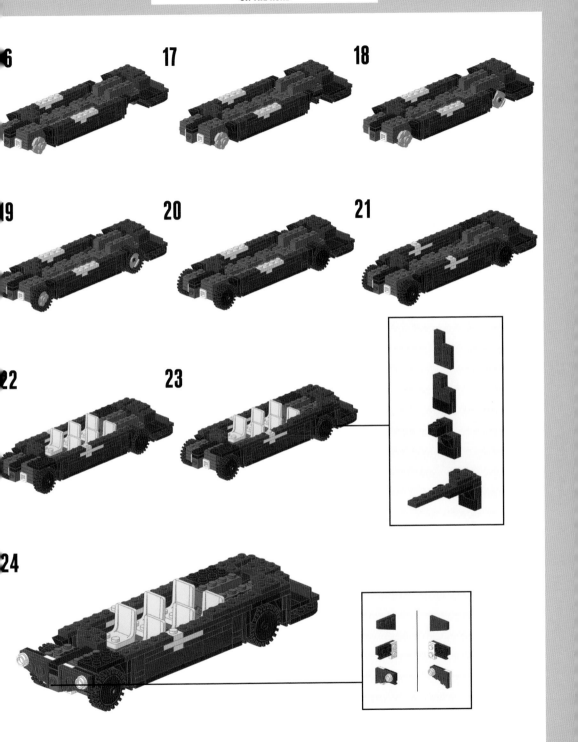

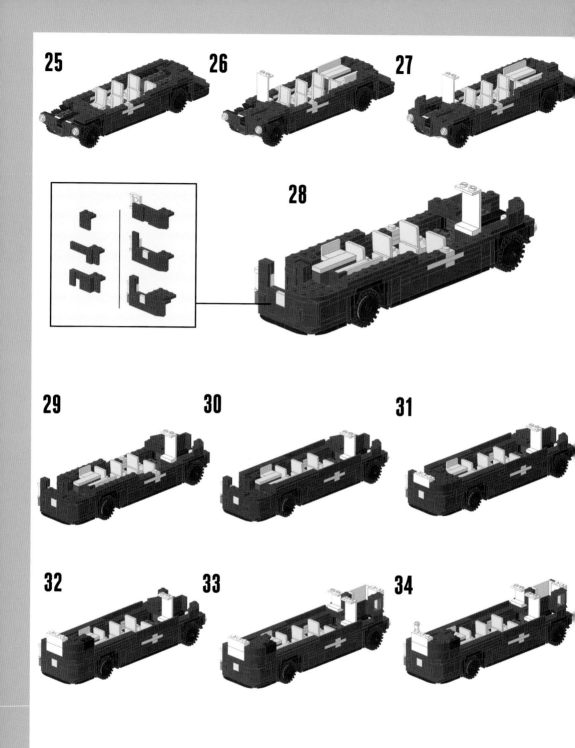

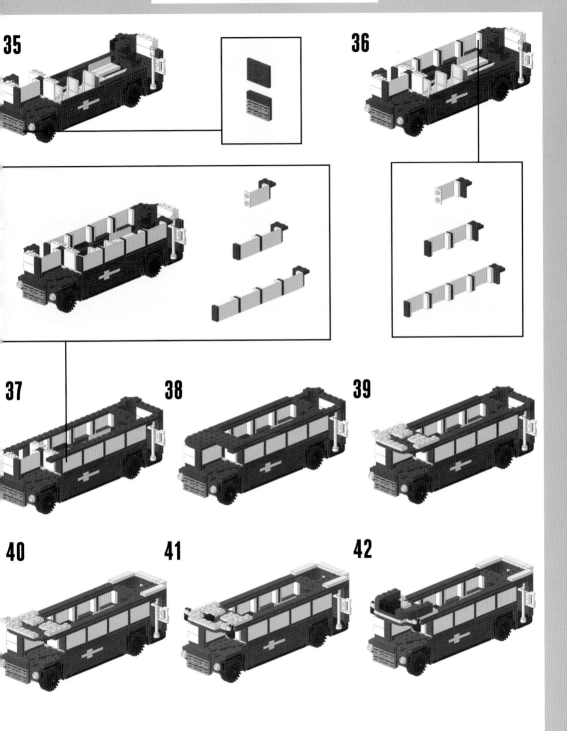

35

36

37

38

39

40

41

42

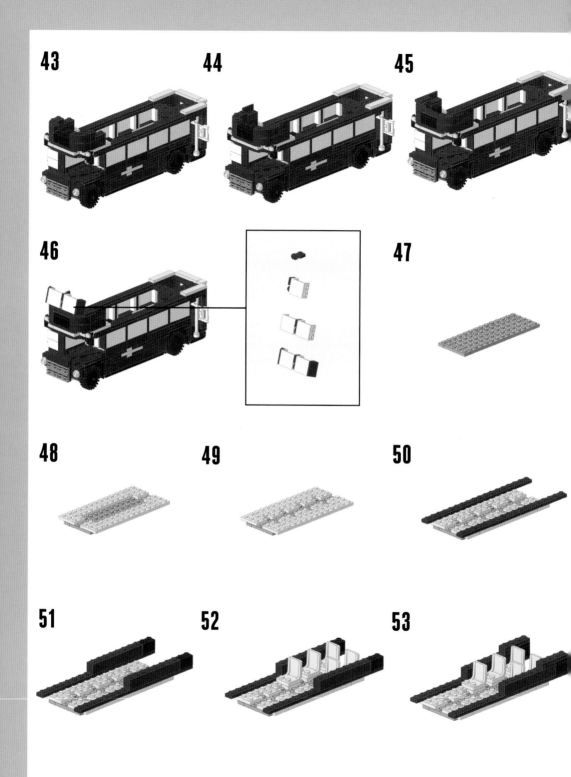

54

55

56

57

58

59

60

61

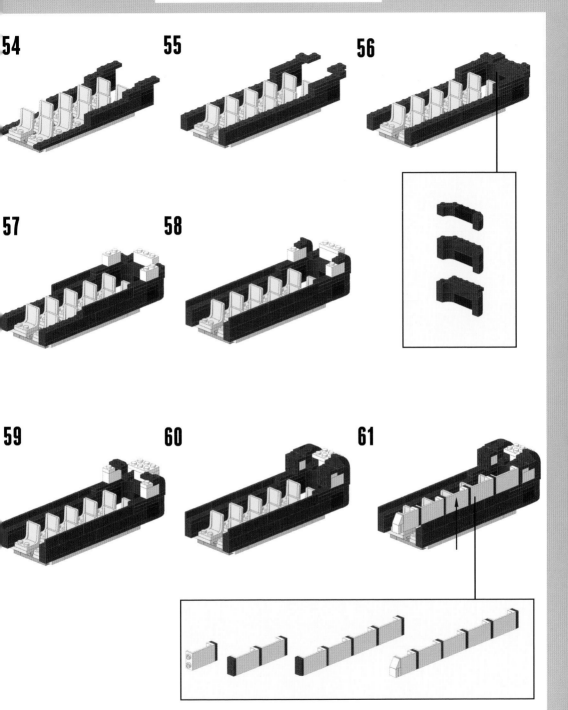

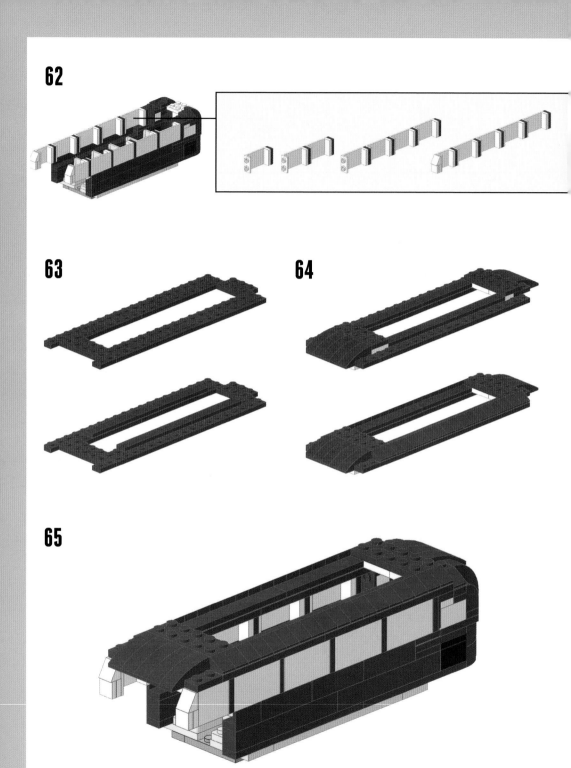

62

63

64

65

66

67

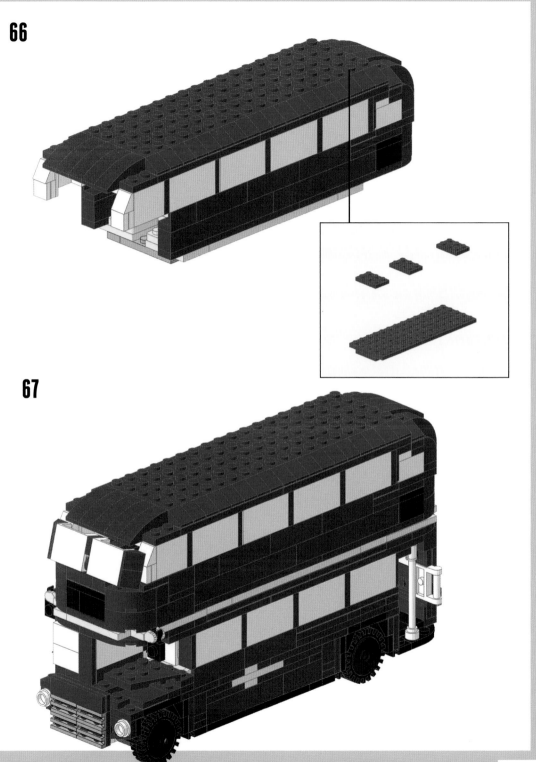

4 x 4 VEHICLE

If you're going off-road, then you'll need a 4 x 4. They have four wheels, all of which are able to be driven. A special connection, called a differential, ensures that although the power is supplied to all four wheels, they can rotate at different speeds. So when the car goes around a corner, the inside wheels are able to travel less than the outside wheels.

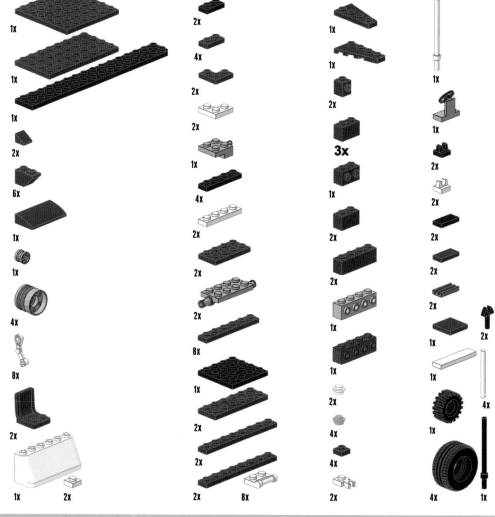

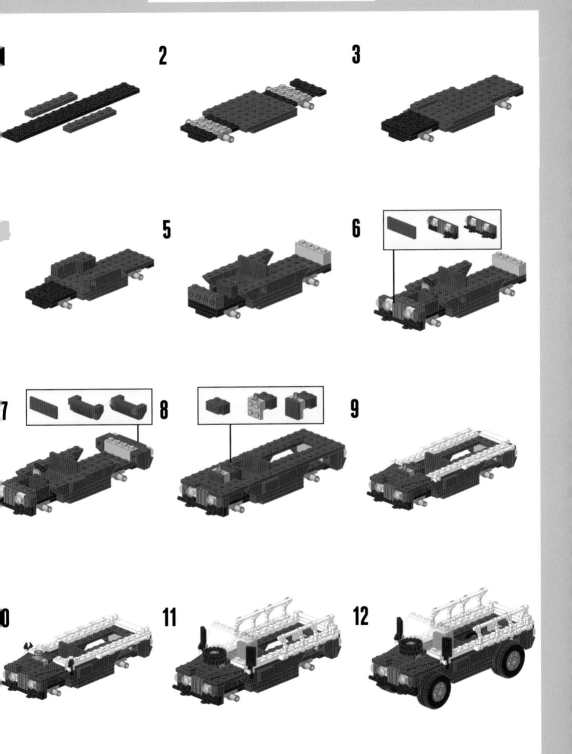

p® is one of the most famous brands of 4 x 4 vehicles. They were first produced in 1941 in Ohio, U.S.A., and were
ginally used as military vehicles during World War II, after which they soon became popular with civilians in many
untries around the world. There are now many different models made under license by several manufacturers, and the
mpany has been owned by various larger companies over the years. Today Jeeps are still used in the military
d remain one of the world's most popular off-road vehicles.

SCHOOL BUS

School buses are instantly
recognizable for a reason. Strict
rules governing the design and
particularly the color of the buses
mean that they are hard to miss.
Safety features such as emergency
doors, special blind-spot mirrors,
and a side-mounted "STOP"
sign ensure that children are
transported to school—and more
importantly, home again—as safely
as possible!

REFUELING TRUCK

Whereas some airports have special fuel lines built into the concrete apron that planes park on, in many cases airplanes have to be refueled by tankers. Airplanes store their fuel in the wings, so towing a set of steps behind the tanker is the easiest way for our driver to access the tanks. Just make sure not to fasten your seatbelt until the refueling is finished.

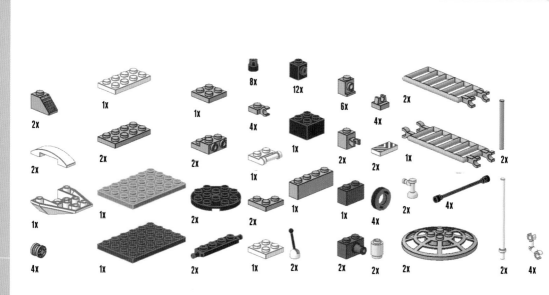

1

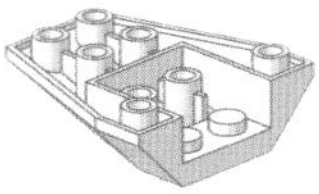

2

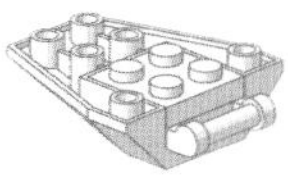

3

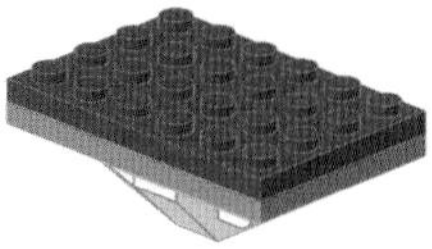

4

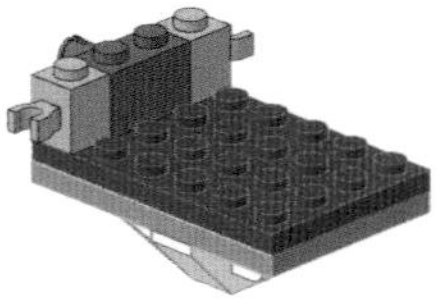

5

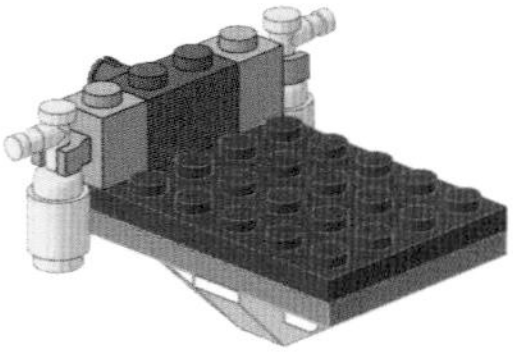

6

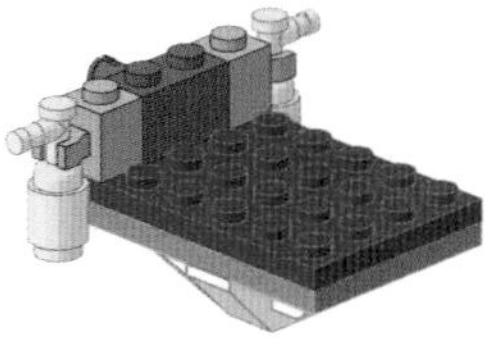

7

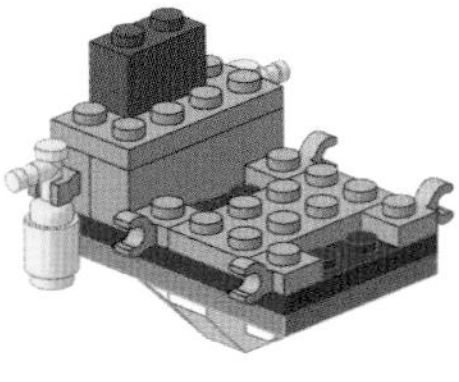

8

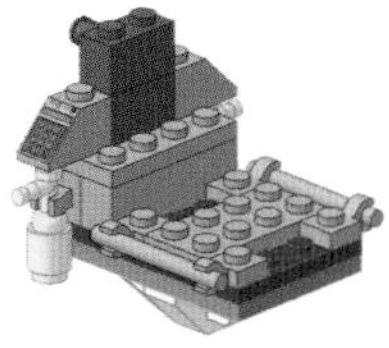

9

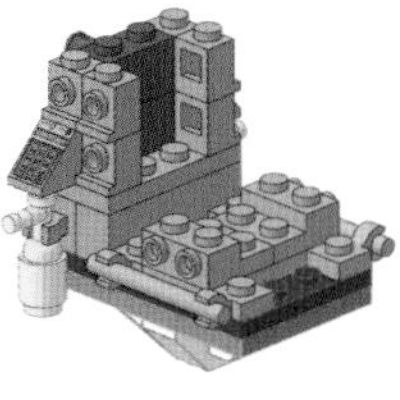

10

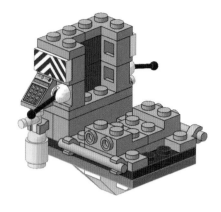

11

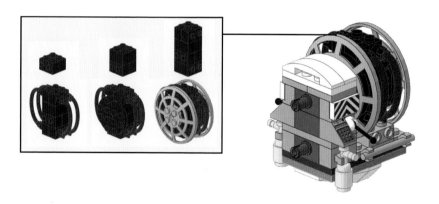

12

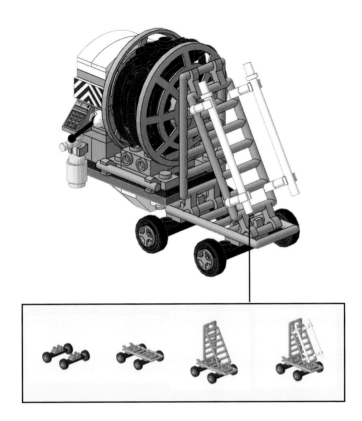

13

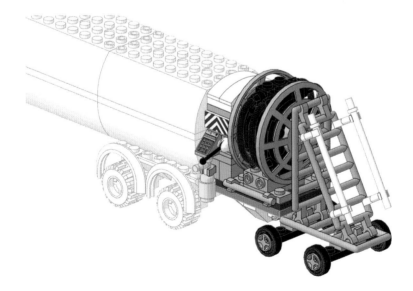

CITROËN 2CV

1948, Paris, France

Britain had the MINI, Germany the Volkswagen Beetle, and France the Citroën 2CV—a low-cost people's car that could be used by anyone for anything. The 2CV had many loyal followers who appreciated its unique styling and straightforward construction. A wide variety of models were made, including many van models, during its 40 years of production. Before 1960, 2CVs were so popular that Citroën spent almost no money on marketing at all—they could easily sell every car that they made! In 1990, 2CV production finally stopped—not until more than 3.8 million of them had been made, though!

Vespa® Scooter

1946, Florence, Italy

Vespa scooters are made by one company only—Piaggio & C. SpA in Italy. In Italian, the word Vespa means "wasp," which makes sense if you have ever heard this scooter! Small, light, and easy to wind around lanes, they work perfectly in Italy, which is still the largest purchaser of Vespas. The small motorcycle has its engine transmission directly connected to the rear wheel, meaning there is no messy chain to worry about. They were also popular in the United Kingdom as part of the 1960s Rockers movement, and today they are seeing a resurgence as an easy way to get around cities.

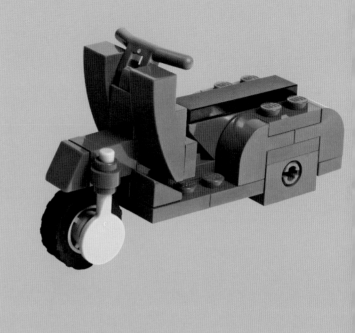

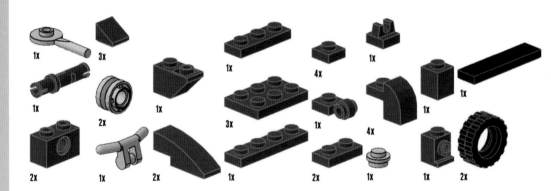

1x 3x 1x 4x 1x 1x

1x 2x 1x 3x 1x 4x 1x

2x 1x 2x 1x 2x 1x 1x 2x

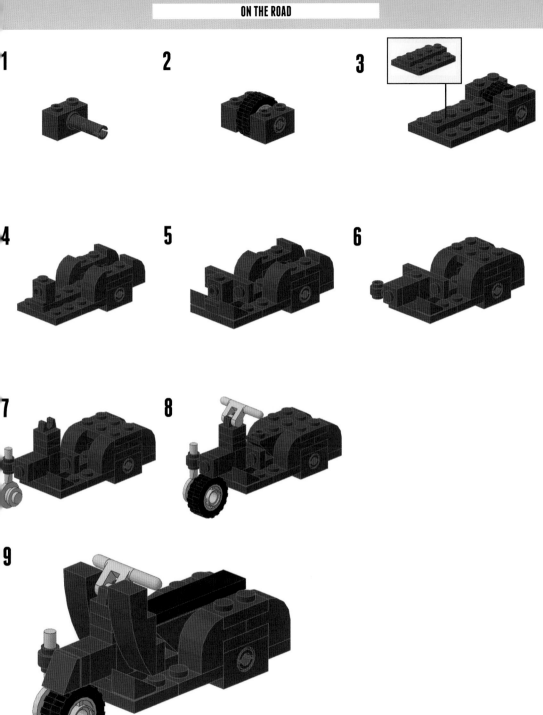

MINI COOPER

1961, Surrey, England

An icon of the swinging '60s, the MINI was designed by Alec Issigonis to be a small family car that would be fuel efficient and cheap to run. A sportier version was created by John Cooper, and this new MINI Cooper was successful as a rally car because of its power and handling. It also featured heavily in the 1969 film *The Italian Job* and its 2003 remake, and the model here is Mr. Bean's famous green MINI with him riding on top. The original MINI lasted until the year 2000, when the new owners of BMW introduced the new MINI that is still on sale today.

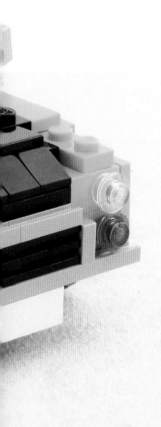

DIGGER

Known in the United Kingdom as a "JCB," in the United States and elsewhere this vehicle is known as a "Backhoe." The reason for this? Just like the "hoover" (vacuum cleaner), the JCB® company was the first to introduce this versatile machine to the United Kingdom, and the name just stuck. With a bucket on a flexible mounting, the backhoe can easily dig trenches, but swap out the bucket and the machine can act like a small crane, auger, or hydraulic breaker—the list goes on. The JCB company even maintains a group of "dancing diggers" that use their complex machinery to perform synchronized dance movements!

SEMI-TRAILER TRUCK

A common sight on most highways is the semi-trailer truck. For maximum flexibility, these vehicles consist of two components—the tractor unit and the trailer. Bending in the middle allows them to navigate tight turns and city streets. There are hundreds of thousands of semi-trailer trucks on the road at any one time, carrying everything that fills the shelves of our local grocery stores. Strict rules apply to semi-trailer truck drivers, though, and they are only allowed to drive for a set amount of time before they must rest. Thankfully this semi-trailer truck is a "sleeper cab" with a bed behind the driver's seat.

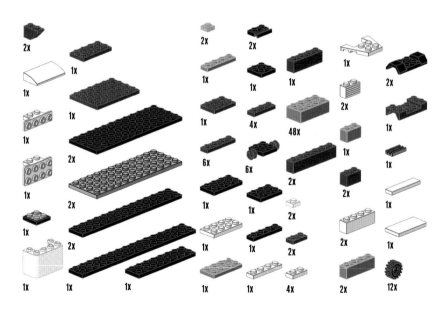

1

2

3

4

5

6

7

8

9

10

11

12

13

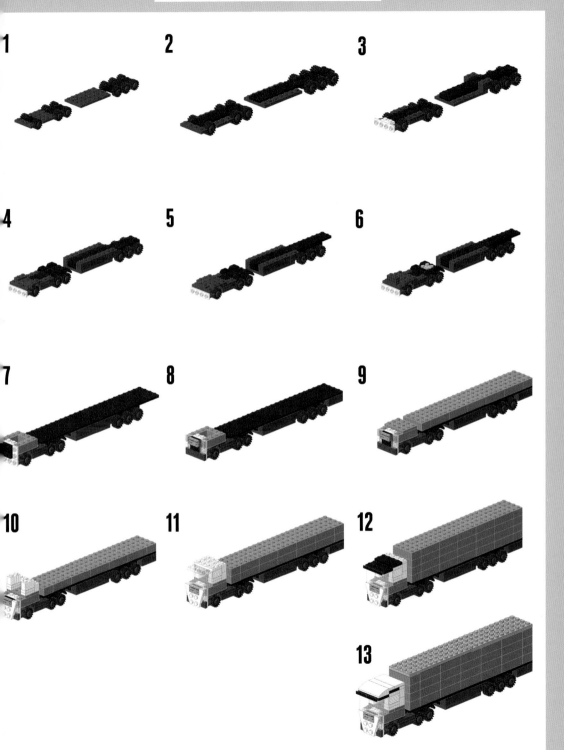

RACING CAR

Formula One (F1) racing cars are built for one thing—speed. Reaching speeds of more than 200 mph (322 kph) and exerting more than 5Gs of force on their drivers in tight turns, it's a complex and dangerous sport. Formula One racing started in 1950, and each year the rules that the cars must adhere to (the "Formula") slightly change. This has led to a variety of car designs throughout the years—some even have six wheels. Most major motor manufacturers have been involved with F1 at one point or another because the extreme racing conditions help companies develop new materials and techniques. This model is based on a 2007 Ferrari.

1 **2** **3**

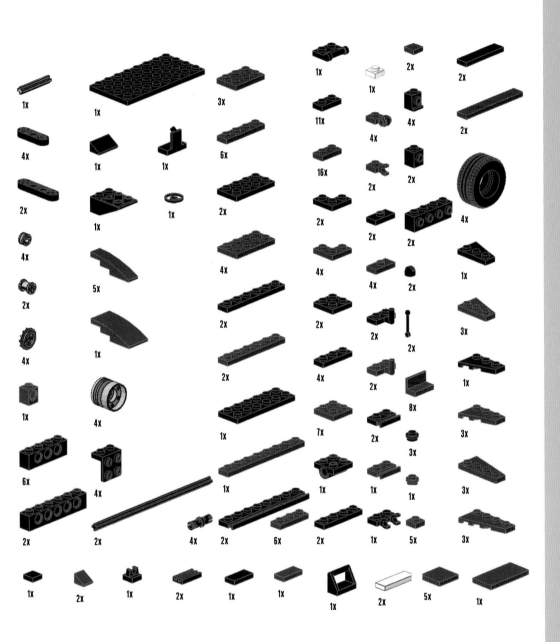

1x 1x 3x 1x 2x 2x

4x 1x 1x 6x 11x 4x 4x 2x

2x 1x 1x 2x 16x 2x 2x 4x

4x 5x 2x 4x 4x 4x 2x 1x

2x 2x 2x 2x 2x 3x

4x 1x 2x 4x 2x 8x 1x

1x 4x 1x 7x 2x 3x 3x

6x 4x 1x 1x 1x 1x 3x

2x 2x 4x 2x 6x 2x 1x 5x 3x

1x 2x 1x 2x 1x 1x 1x 2x 5x 1x

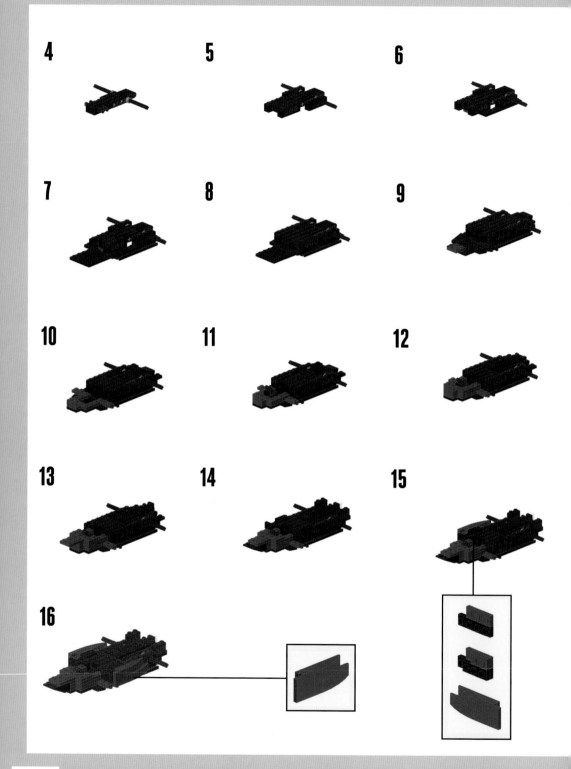

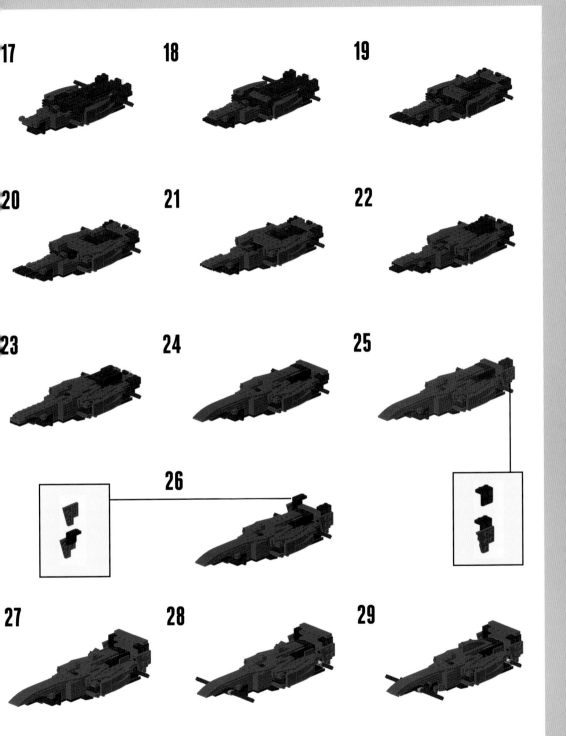

30

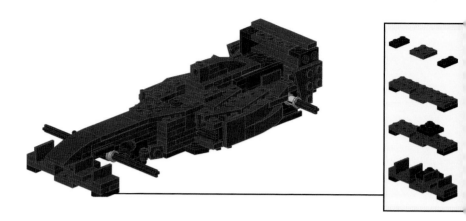

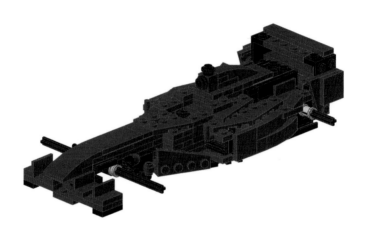

31

32

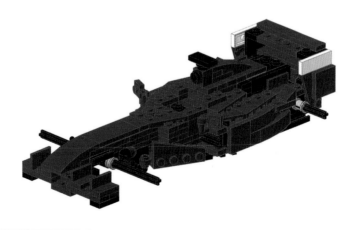

33

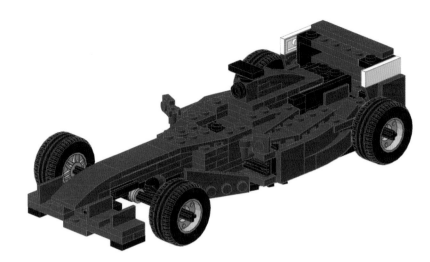

34

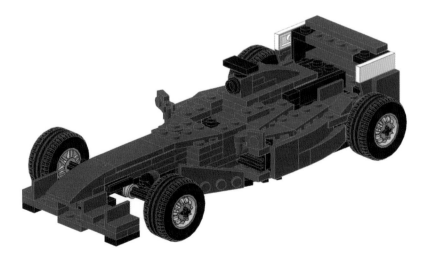

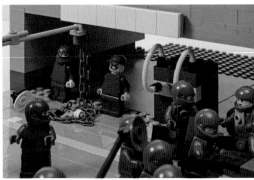

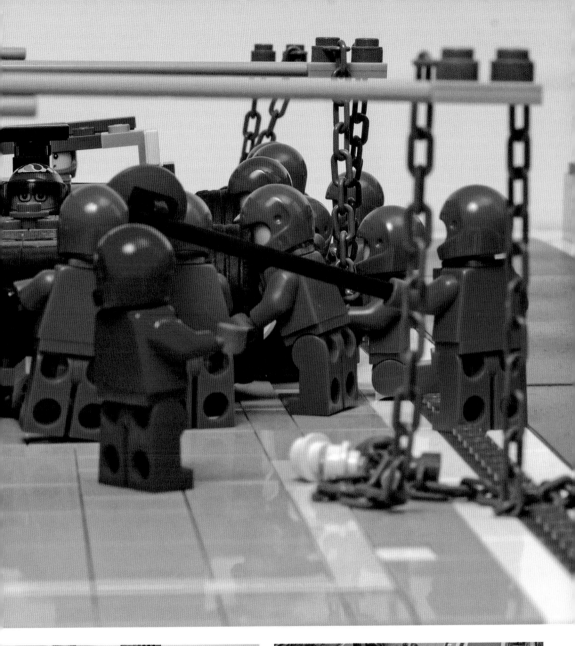

TOW TRUCK

Hopefully you'll never need one of these when out and about on your wheels, but if all else fails when you're on the road, it's good to know that there is a tow truck out there to help you. These trucks have specially designed platforms on the back that can be lowered down to the ground. A powerful winch then pulls your car up on top of the truck so it can be taken home. At least replacing a LEGO® wheel is easier than replacing the real thing!

VW Camper Van

Did you know that the VW Camper Van is now over 60 years old? Depending on where you live in the world, you might call it a VW Bus, Kombi, Microbus, or Transporter, but whatever the name, it's a highly recognizable vehicle! Believe it or not, production of this iconic vehicle continued until 2003 in Brazil. Descendants of this model are still produced, but none have the characteristic shapes and curves of the original, which was created at the German VW Wolfsburg factory from Beetle parts. As a result, they were deceptively small vehicles that would actually fit inside some modern vans!

LUNAR ROVER

The first car designed to be used outside Earth was the Apollo Lunar Roving Vehicle. Battery driven and with only two seats, it was used on Apollos 15, 16, and 17 to explore the surface of the moon. It's likely that the Lunar Rover was one of the most expensive cars ever produced, with a bill of $38 million, although it did come with some very advanced features, including a remote-controlled color video camera. A total of four Lunar Rovers were made—of which three are still on the moon. The fourth Rover never made the journey and was used for spare parts after the Apollo 18 mission was canceled.

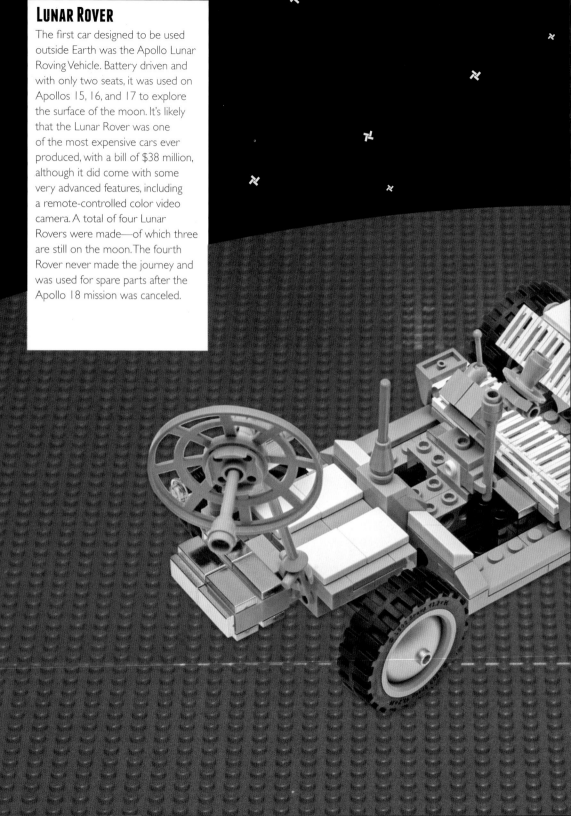

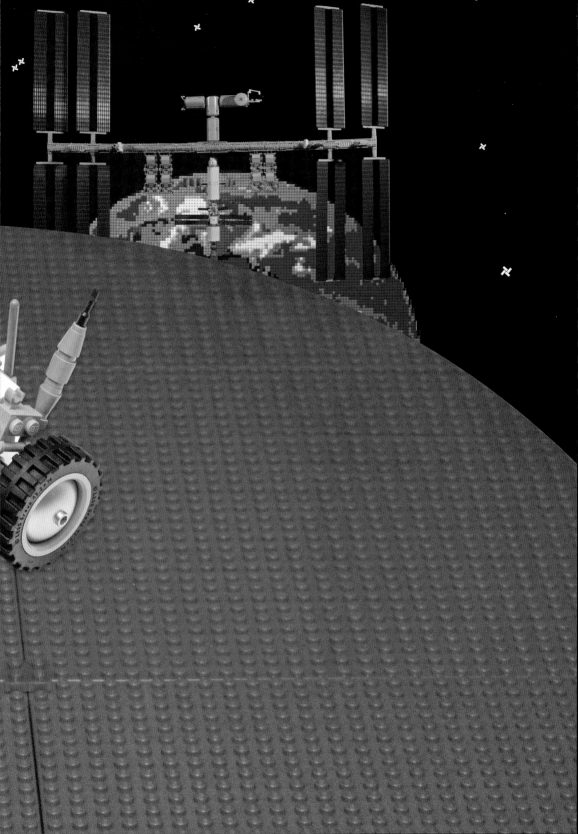

OFF THE RAILS

STEAM TRAIN

There is something special about steam trains, such as this one in the picturesque town of Neuffen, Germany. Although most modern Western services are now diesel or electric, steam trains still evoke a certain feeling for their passengers. Using coal, wood, or oil fire, steam trains heat water into steam that pushes the pistons that, in turn, drive the wheels. Although the use of steam locomotives for general services went into decline at the start of the twentieth century, most countries still retain their steam locomotives for heritage railroads or special services. In fact, steam traction is so popular that the United Kingdom built a brand-new steam engine in 2009.

Photograph © Ronald Vallenduuk

STEAM LOCOMOTIVE

19th century, Great Britain

This little steam locomotive should be easy enough for any LEGO® train enthusiast to build. I've used a few special pieces in this model to let me build the boiler and cab sideways. It's an easy way to take advantage of the round pieces available. Why not try building a few carriages for this little train to pull around yourself?

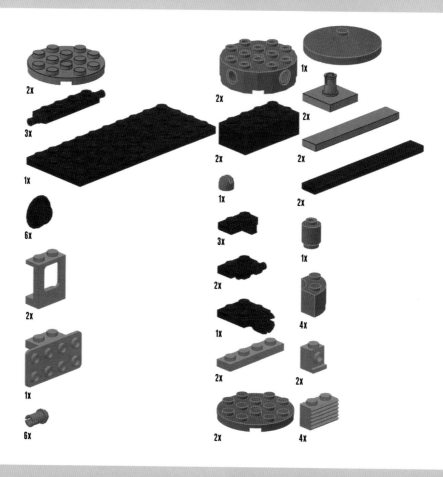

2

3

4

5

6

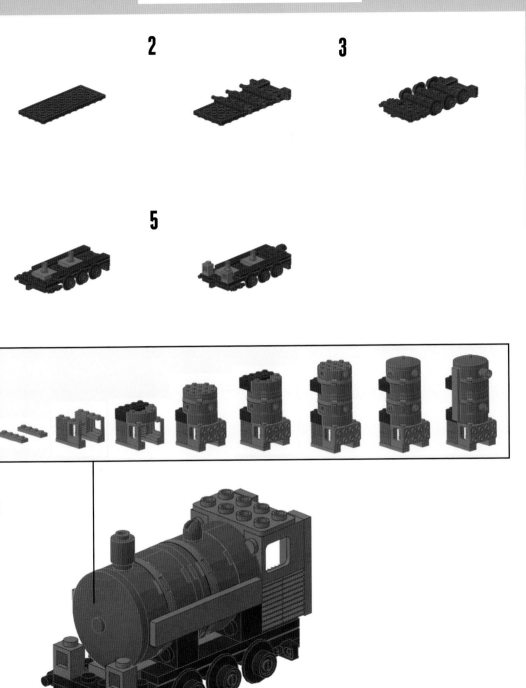

ROLLER COASTER

If you want to have fun on the rails, there's no better way than on a roller coaster! While they might look scary, roller coasters are actually very carefully designed to be as safe as possible. Otherwise visitors wouldn't come back! Our little coaster is a good example. The two sets of wheels wrap around the track (flexible tubing in our model) to make sure that the car can't come off the rails. The lap bars ensure that our minifigures don't fall out as they go around the corners. Hold tight!

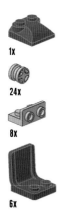
1x

24x

8x

6x

1x

1x

2x

3x

3x

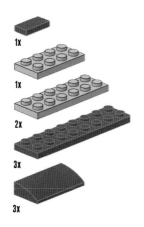
1x

12x

2x

2x

5x

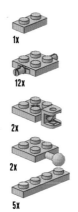
2x

1x

1x

3x

3x

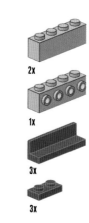

6x

2x

2x

12x

1

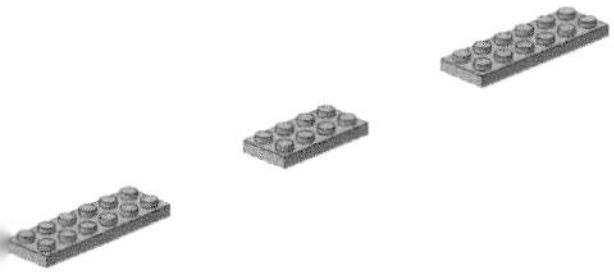

2

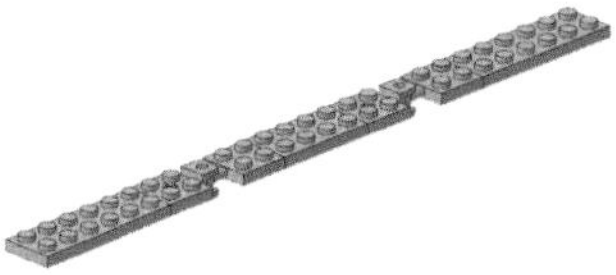

3

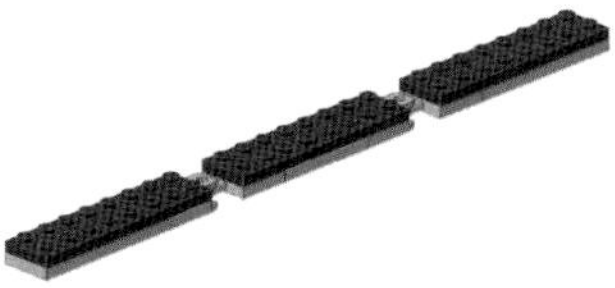

4

5

6

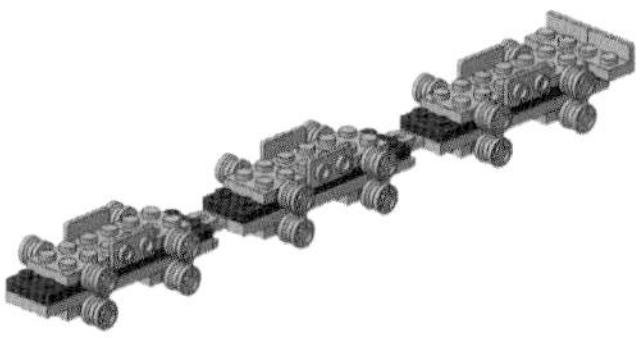

7

8

9

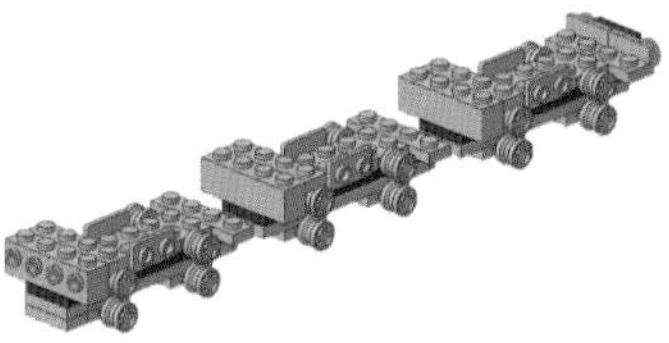

10

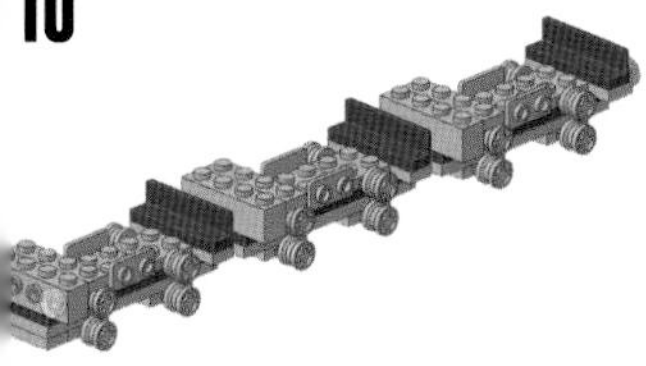

11

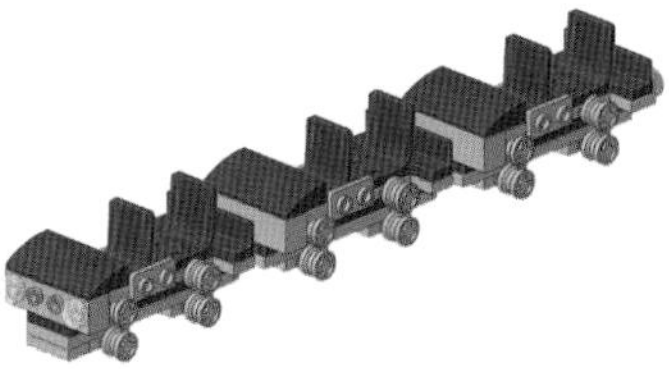

12

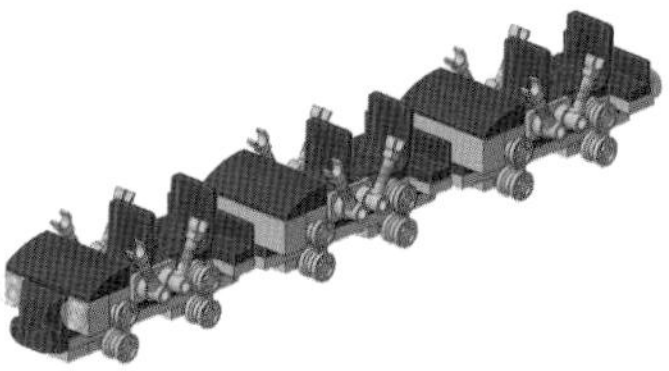

13

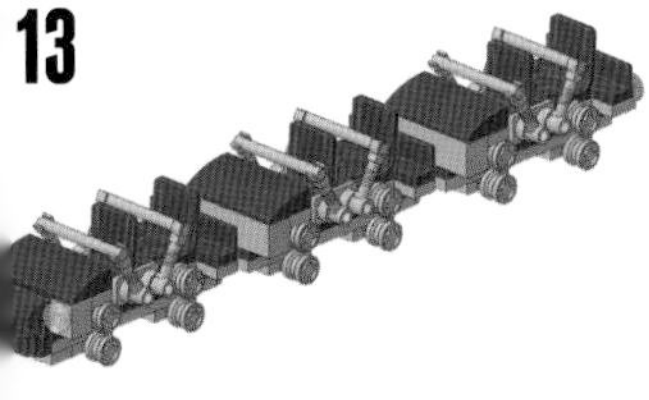

LONDON UNDERGROUND TRAIN

While it's known simply as "the Tube" to Londoners, did you know that more than half of the London Underground is actually above ground? The first part of the Underground was constructed by a private company and opened in 1863—making it the world's oldest underground railroad. Throughout the years, other companies dug their own tunnels to create their own underground lines. It wasn't until 1933 that these companies were merged to create the network that we know today. The network isn't static though. The last major expansion was to the Jubilee line in 1999, extending it to what is now the Olympic Park in east London.

Stephenson's Rocket

1829, Newcastle upon Tyne, England

The Rocket wasn't the first railroad locomotive built, but it's one of the most famous! It was designed by Robert Stephenson and included a number of new features that were never seen before, such as multiple boiler fire-tubes to heat the water faster and a more powerful engine. The pistons were also mounted more horizontally and directly drove the wheels. You might find that the wheels are quite hard to get a hold of in yellow, but don't worry—brown wheels will work just as well.

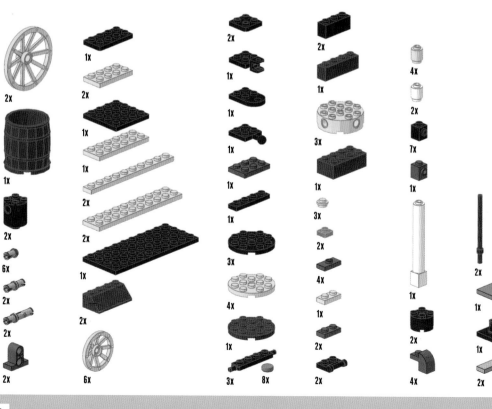

1

2

3

4

5

6

7

8

9

10

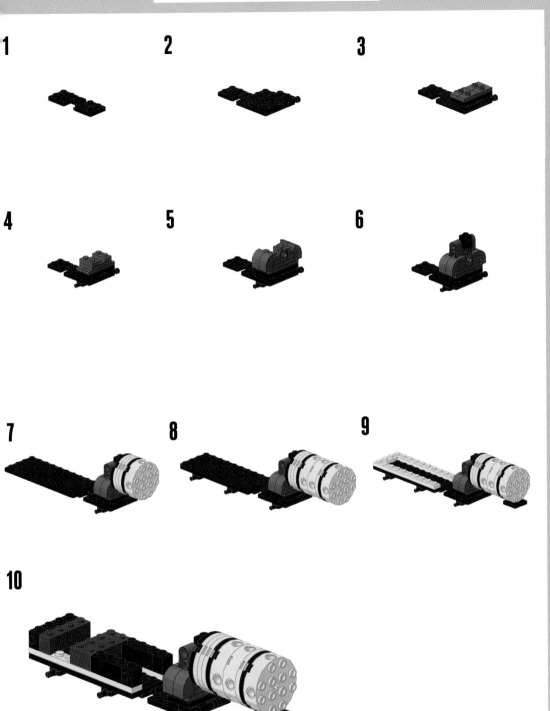

11

12

13

14

15

16

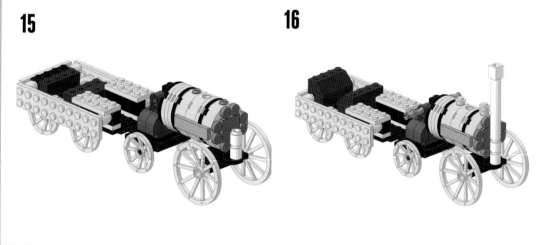

17

18

FUNICULAR

Whereas most traditional railroads use smooth wheels, a funicular railroad is pulled by a cable. In fact, most funicular railroads have two cars—each attached to the same cable and counterbalancing their weight. Using a cable means that funicular railroads are capable of operating on very steep hills—the steepest in use today is in Australia and has a grade of 52 degrees! This model is of the funicular railroad in Lisbon, Portugal. It opened in 1885 and was declared a national monument in 2002.

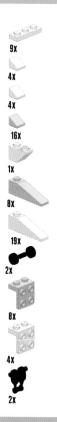

9x
4x
4x
16x
1x
8x
19x
2x
8x
4x
2x

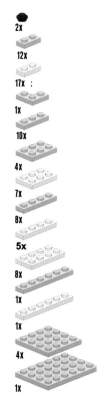

2x
12x
17x :
1x
10x
4x
7x
8x
5x
8x
1x
1x
4x
1x

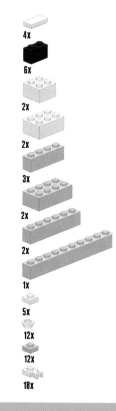

4x
6x
2x
2x
3x
2x
2x
1x
5x
12x
12x
18x

2x
4x
17x
2x
2x
2x
2x
4x
2x
5x

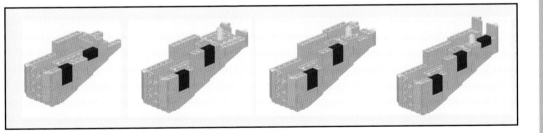

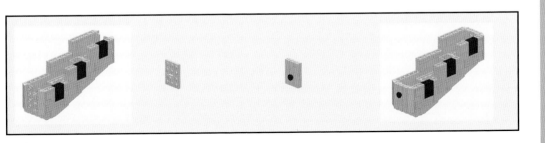

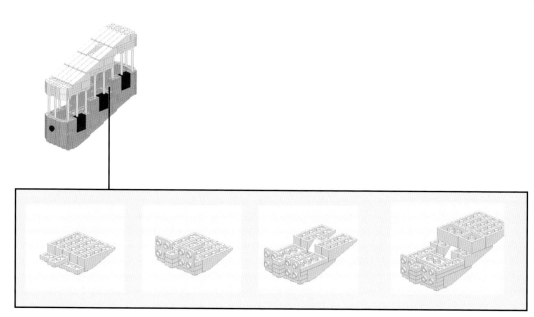

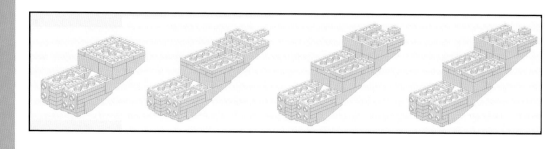

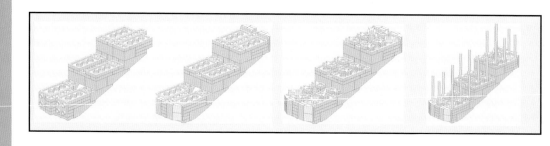

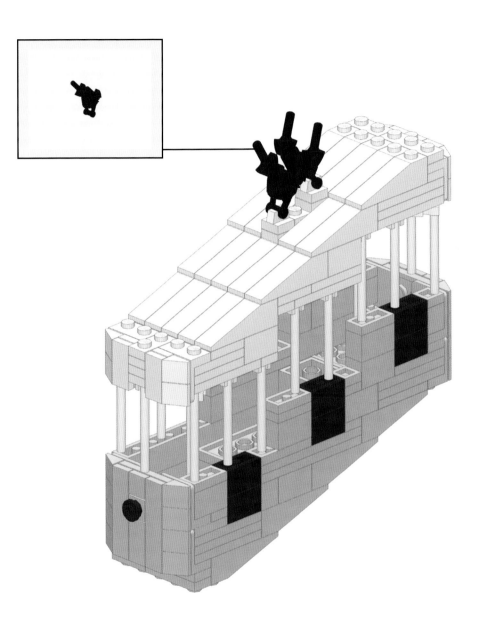

SEASIDE TRAM

The Blackpool tramway is one of the oldest in the world, dating back to 1885. It is the only "seaside" (as it is called in the United Kingdom) tram system that has remained in use ever since it was opened, most likely because of the continuous tourist trade! Although the Blackpool system now runs modern step-free trams, they have wisely kept the traditional designs that have been around for much longer. Balloon cars built in the 1930s run alongside cars such as this Coronation car introduced in 1953, the year of Queen Elizabeth II's coronation.

NARROW-GAUGE TRAIN

As the name suggests, a narrow-gauge railroad has a narrower gauge—the distance between the tracks. Shortening this distance brings some real advantages—trains, tracks, and bridges are cheaper to build, and the railroad can reach places that a normal-sized railroad couldn't. Our narrow-gauge train is based on those used by slate mines. The smaller engines and trucks could be used inside the mines, and it wasn't uncommon for them to be so small that the driver had to sit sideways.

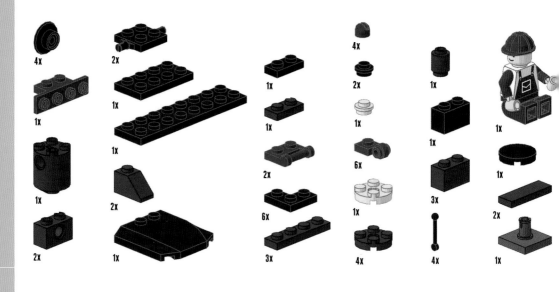

4x
2x
1x
1x
1x
2x
2x
1x

1x
1x
1x
2x
6x
3x

4x
2x
1x
6x
1x
4x

1x
1x
1x
3x
4x

1x
1x
2x
1x

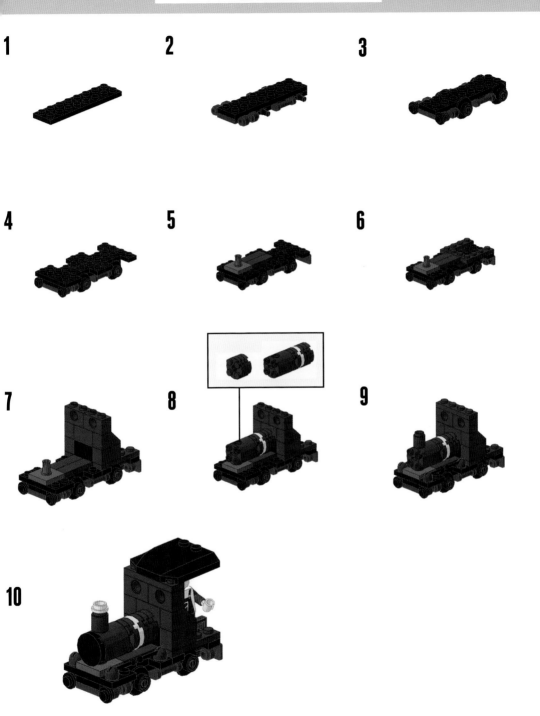

FREIGHT TRAIN

If you have a lot of freight to move
across country, then this is the way
to do it. Trains were first developed
to move freight—usually coal—and
have been moving it ever since. This
train is based on a 1960s British Rail
Class 25 model used in the north
of England. In certain parts of the
world, it is still more common to
see a freight train than one carrying
passengers, though the number
of passenger trains has increased.
Today's coal wagons may weigh up
to 130 tons. Some trains are now
so long that they require multiple
engines and can stretch to more
than a mile (1.6 km) long!

RAILROAD HANDCAR

How do you get around a railroad if there's no engine? One of these might help. This is a handcar, or sometimes a pump car. These were usually used by maintenance crews who needed to move around on the rails. The passengers stood or sat on the platform and moved their arms up and down. Through a series of connecting rods, this powered the wheels and pushed the car along. Whereas these were extremely common in the early days of railroads, they have now almost all been replaced by motorized versions. A few still exist though, and there are a few events where they are even raced!

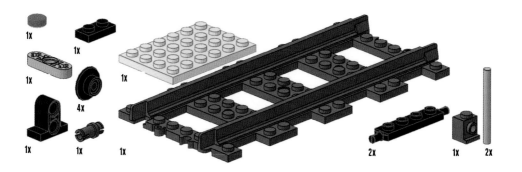

1x
1x
1x
1x
4x
1x
1x
1x
2x
1x
2x

1

2

3

4

5

6

MACHU PICCHU TRAIN

Proving that you don't need any special LEGO® wheels to create a train, this little train is a recreation of the train that climbs up Machu Picchu in Peru. The wheels are made of 2 × 2 round plates. Even the windows are made from transparent plates—no special parts here! This design is easy to follow and adapt to your local trains. Try making the carriages in different colors and see how they look.

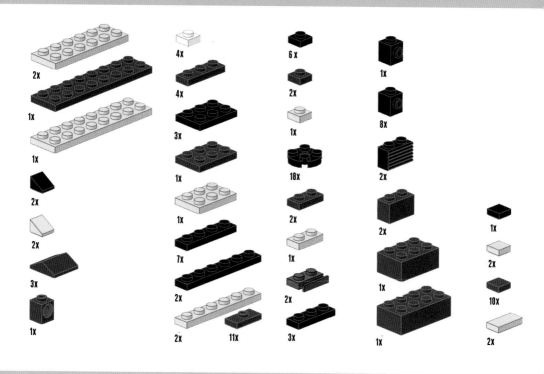

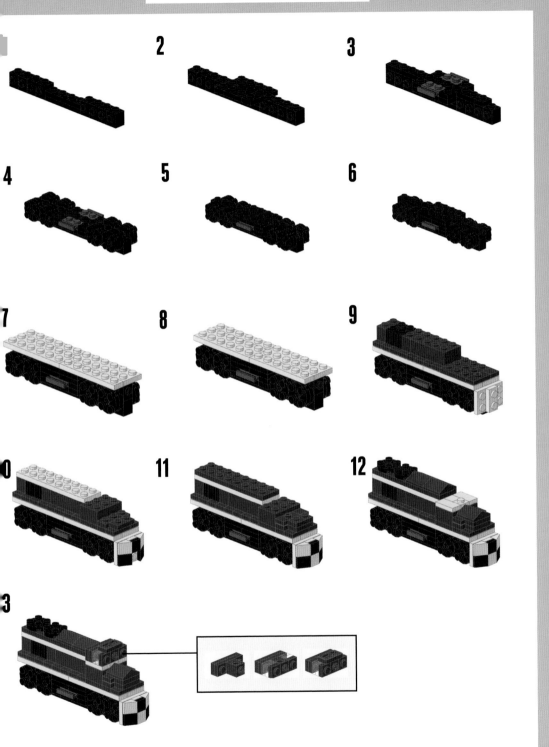

2

3

4

5

6

7

8

9

10

11

12

13

High-speed Train

Running throughout Europe is a
network of high-speed railroads,
regularly exceeding speeds of
170 mph (274 kph). Running
between most European countries,
they rival air transport for speed,
comfort, and, of course, ease of use.
Italy led the way, opening its high-
speed rail in 1977, but it was France
that popularized high-speed rail in
1981 with the TGV (Train à Grand
Vitesse). Germany, Spain, Belgium,
and the Netherlands all followed
suit, connecting their railroads to
slash journey times across Europe.
Europe's high-speed trains are
constantly being upgraded, with the
latest trains able to exceed 350 mph
(563 kph)—faster than a small plane.

WALT DISNEY WORLD® MONORAIL

1971, Florida, U.S.A.

This type of transport only has one rail to work on—that's why it's called a monorail, from the Greek word "monos," which means "alone." This type of monorail is in use at theme parks and in small cities—you might have seen it when on vacation. The car runs on top of a large concrete beam that can be elevated above the ground. This makes running the monorail above rivers, roads, and trees very easy. They can also give you a great view of your journey and don't take up too much space.

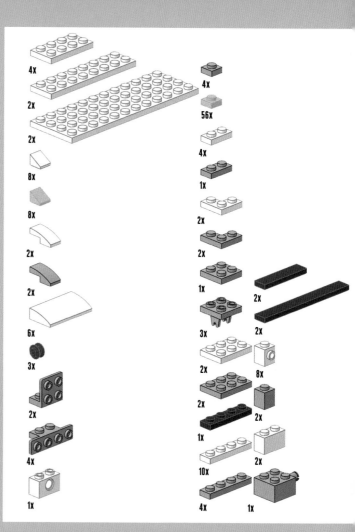

4x
2x
2x
8x
8x
2x
2x
6x
3x
2x
4x
1x

4x
56x
4x
1x
2x
2x
1x
3x
2x
2x
1x
10x
4x

2x
2x
8x
2x
2x
1x

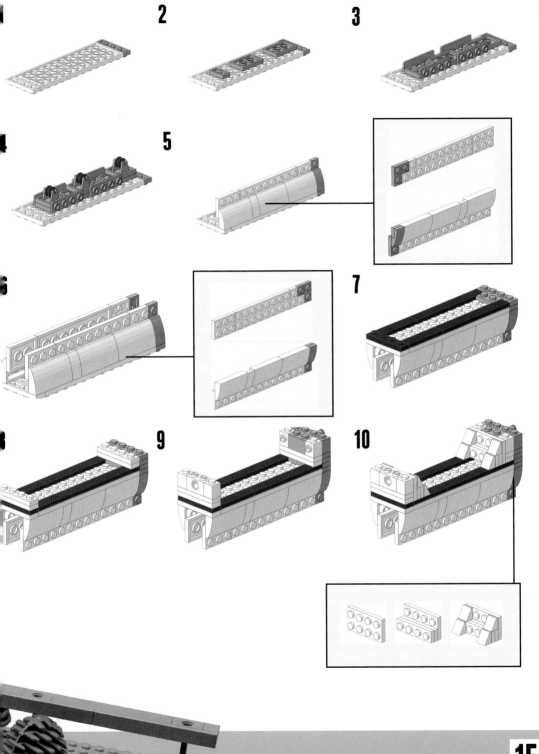

11

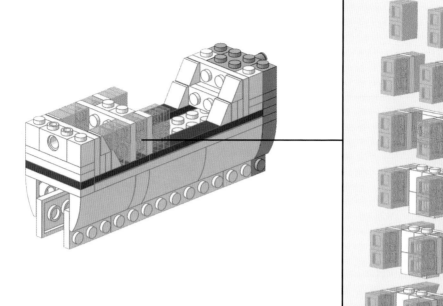

12

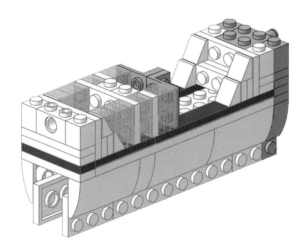

13

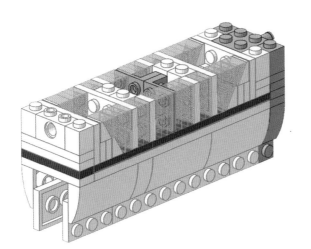

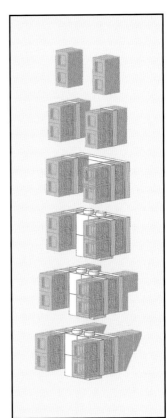

14

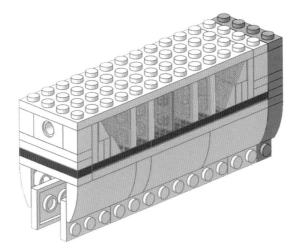

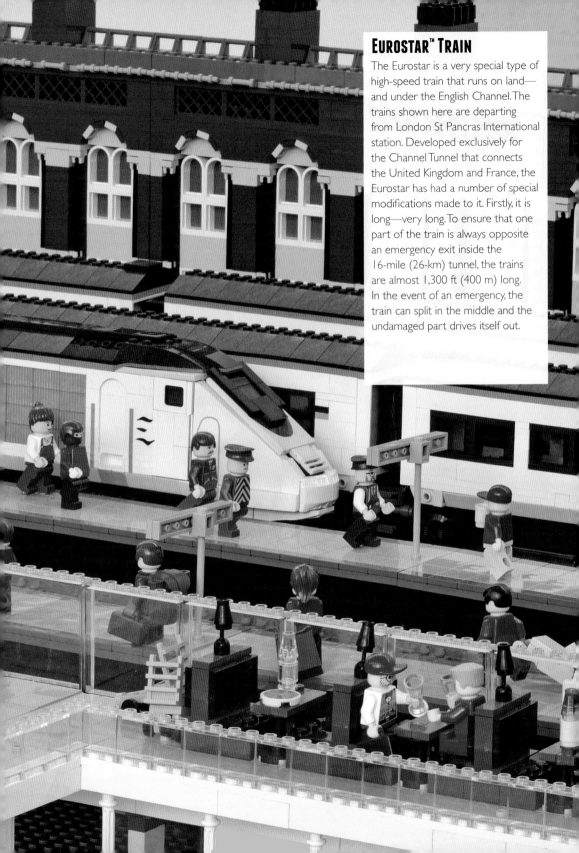

EUROSTAR™ TRAIN

The Eurostar is a very special type of high-speed train that runs on land—and under the English Channel. The trains shown here are departing from London St Pancras International station. Developed exclusively for the Channel Tunnel that connects the United Kingdom and France, the Eurostar has had a number of special modifications made to it. Firstly, it is long—very long. To ensure that one part of the train is always opposite an emergency exit inside the 16-mile (26-km) tunnel, the trains are almost 1,300 ft (400 m) long. In the event of an emergency, the train can split in the middle and the undamaged part drives itself out.

MAKING WAVES

CRUISE SHIP

1969, Southampton, England

If you are going on a journey, why not enjoy the traveling as much as the destination? That's the idea behind a cruise ship. A floating hotel, the modern cruise ship ranks among some of the largest ships in use today. On board ships such as this RMS *Queen Mary 2*, you'll find fine dining, casinos, and swimming pools. Many large cruise ships are so big that they can't dock in some of the locations that they visit. Smaller tenders are used to transfer passengers ashore—if you can bear to tear yourself away!

Photography © Lars Jockumsen

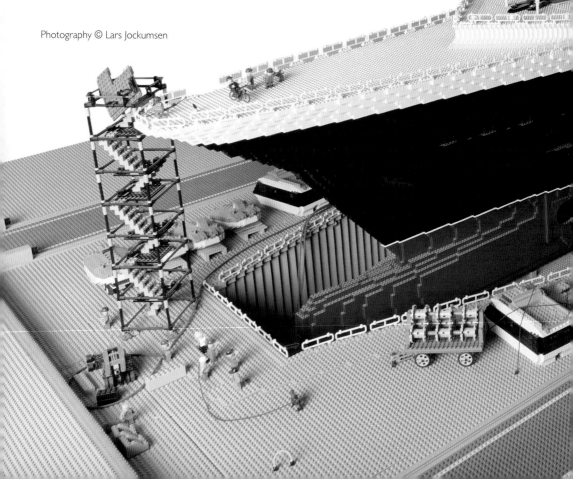

CONTAINER SHIP

It is almost certain that the very book you are reading has spent some time on a container ship—around 90 per cent of the world's trade is taken by container at least for some of the journey. The containers transported by this ship are large metal boxes, built to an international standard. That means that no matter where the ship travels to, it can be unloaded quickly and easily using local equipment. Container ships are measured in twenty-foot equivalent units (TEU). The largest ships operating today have a capacity of more than 18,000 TEU.

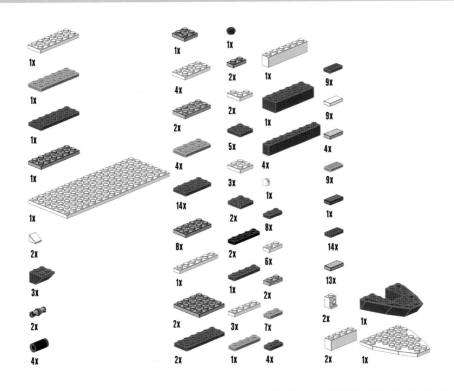

1

2

3

4

5

6

7

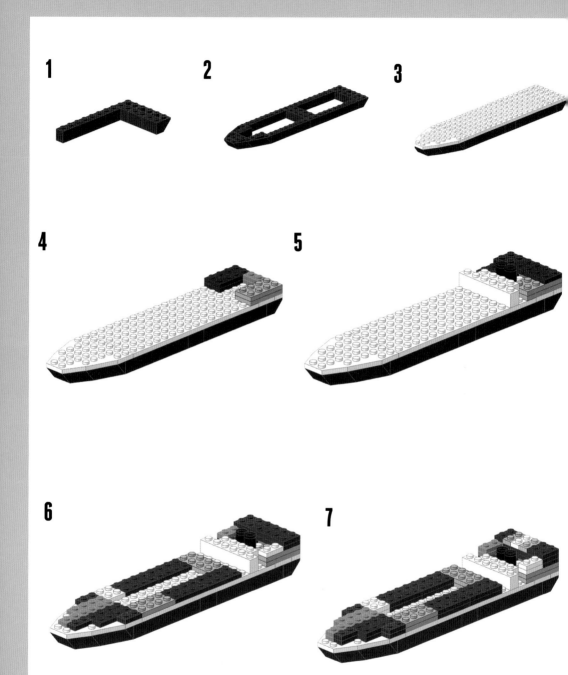

8

9

10

11

12

13

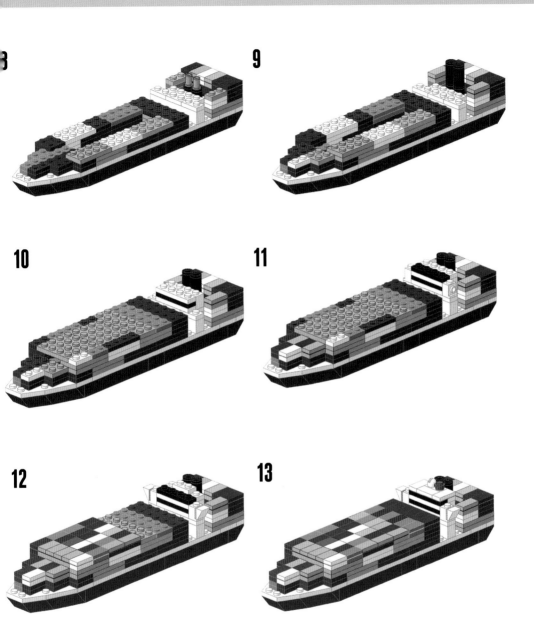

IRONCLAD WARSHIP

Ironclads were an early type of warship. Propelled by a steam engine, they had no sails and a completely covered deck. The iron panels were used to defend the ship against incendiary shells that might otherwise set fire to a wooden ship. Ironclad ships rapidly replaced traditional ships when they were introduced. They were developed so quickly that it was quite common for a brand-new ship to already be considered outdated when it was first launched.

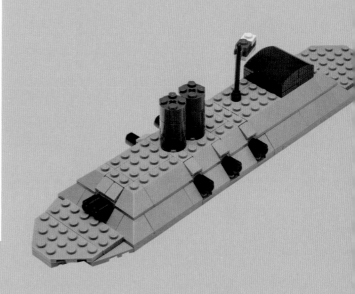

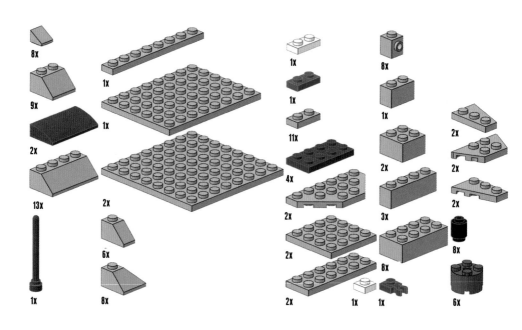

8x

9x

1x

2x

13x

1x

1x

1x

2x

6x

8x

1x

1x

11x

4x

2x

2x

2x

1x

1x

2x

2x

3x

8x

8x

2x

1x

1x

6x

1

2

3

4

5

6

7

8

9

10

11

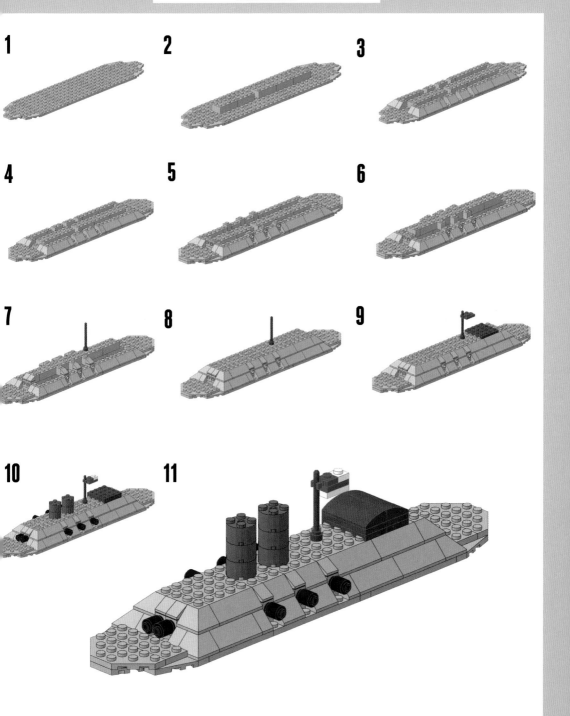

FISHING TRAWLER

The North Sea, located between the United Kingdom and mainland Europe, maintains a large fishing fleet, and many of these boats are trawlers. To catch the fish, a large net is dragged through the water behind the boat. This type of trawler is a beam trawler—the nets are dragged behind from the two booms that swing out sideways. The nets are designed to only catch grown fish, but they can also catch any type of fish. Once caught, it's up to the fishermen to make sure that any fish they don't want are sorted through and returned back to the sea.

NARROWBOAT

Narrowboats are very specific to the United Kingdom as these boats were built to overcome a specific problem. The early transport networks in many countries were based on rivers and canals, so much so that the United Kingdom developed a very extensive network of canals. To move boats up and down the hillside, canal boat locks were built with only a width of 7 ft (2 m). Although originally built for cargo, modern canal boats have almost all been converted into homes or pleasure cruisers. Our narrowboat is also set up to deliver coal to keep people warm in the winter.

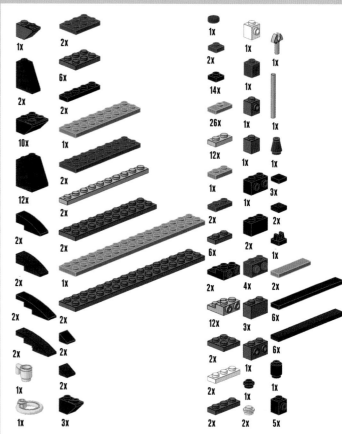

1

2

3

4

5

6

7

8

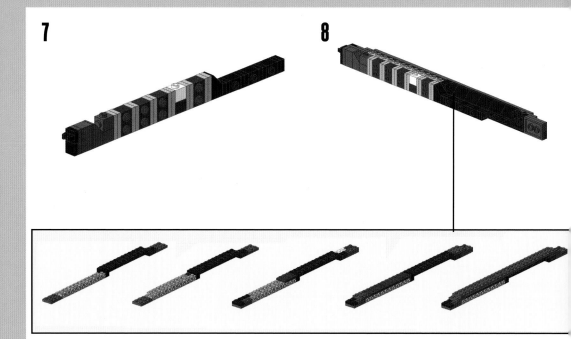

9

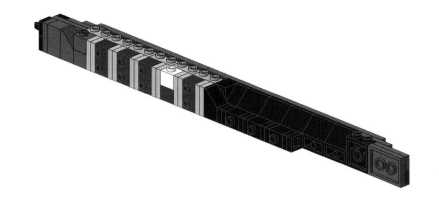

10

11

12

13

14

15

16

17

18

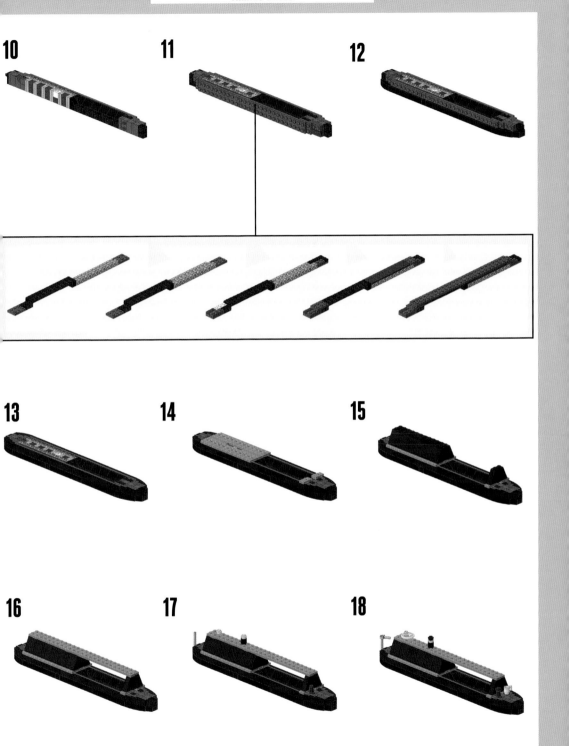

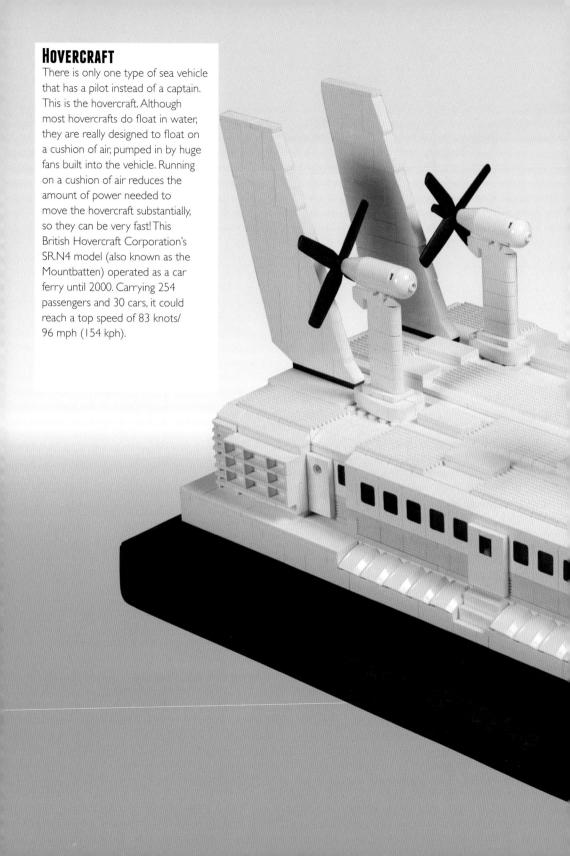

Hovercraft

There is only one type of sea vehicle that has a pilot instead of a captain. This is the hovercraft. Although most hovercrafts do float in water, they are really designed to float on a cushion of air, pumped in by huge fans built into the vehicle. Running on a cushion of air reduces the amount of power needed to move the hovercraft substantially, so they can be very fast! This British Hovercraft Corporation's SR.N4 model (also known as the Mountbatten) operated as a car ferry until 2000. Carrying 254 passengers and 30 cars, it could reach a top speed of 83 knots/ 96 mph (154 kph).

AIRBOAT

Airboats are a special type of ship designed to operate in very shallow or marshy conditions where a propeller might easily get caught. Instead of being pushed along by a propeller, a large fan mounted at the back of the boat provides the power. To steer the airboat, two rudders are usually placed behind the fan to direct the airflow. Although you might immediately think of airboats in the Florida swamps, these boats have been used for many different purposes, including disaster relief and ice rescue.

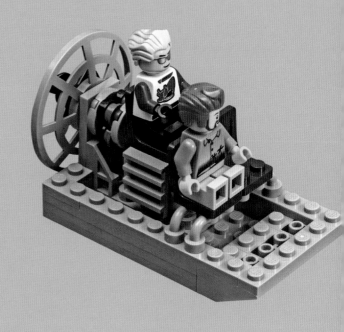

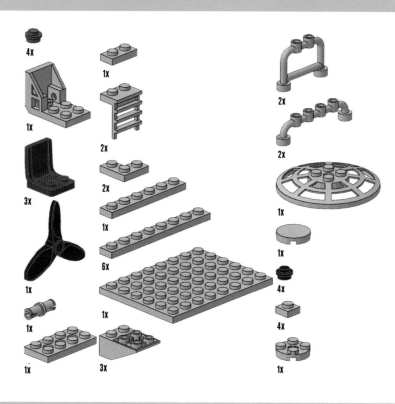

4x

1x

1x

2x

3x

2x

2x

1x

1x

6x

1x

1x

2x

2x

1x

1x

4x

4x

1x

3x

1x

1

2

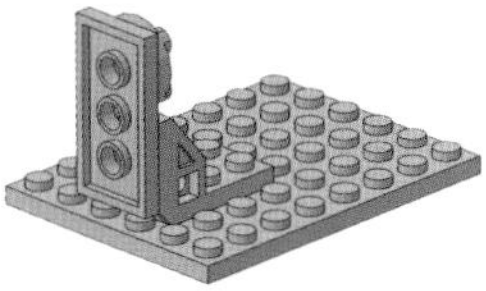

3

4

5

6

7

8

9

10

11

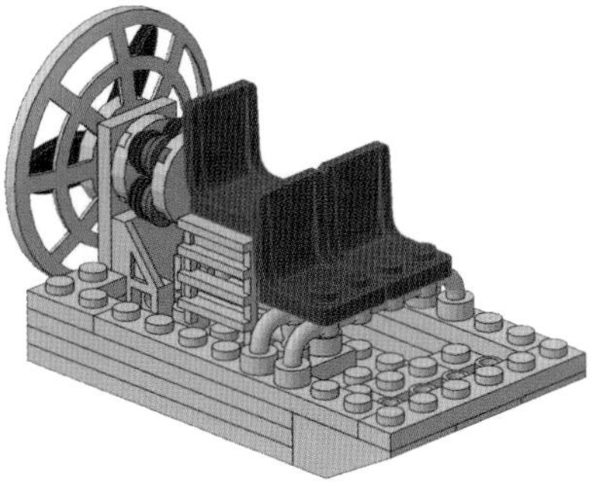

SUBMARINE

One of the few modes of sea transport that is designed to operate under the sea, the modern submarine is a highly sophisticated vessel and can work at great depths. Submarines rise and sink through the water by altering their buoyancy. They do this by pumping water into or out of special ballast tanks. The more water, the heavier the submarine is, and down it goes! When underwater, submarines use a variety of moving surfaces to steer—similar in operation to an airplane. Tilting the planes pushes the passing water up or down, and hence the submarine goes up or down.

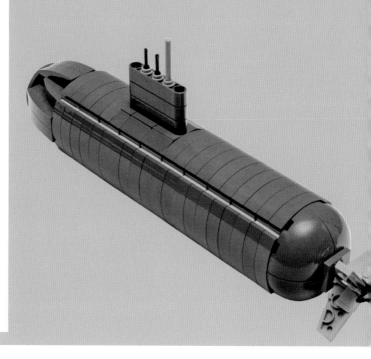

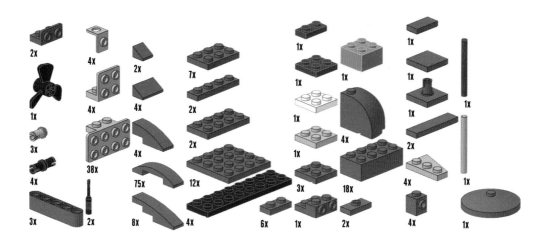

2x   4x   2x   7x   1x   1x   1x   1x   1x

1x   4x   4x   2x   1x   1x   4x   2x   1x

3x   38x   4x   2x   1x

4x   75x   12x   3x   18x   4x   1x

3x   2x   8x   4x   6x   1x   2x   4x   1x

1

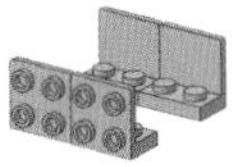

2

3

4

5

6

7

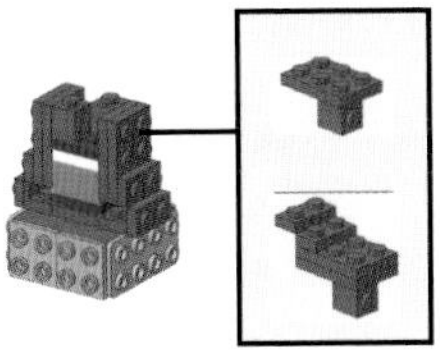

8

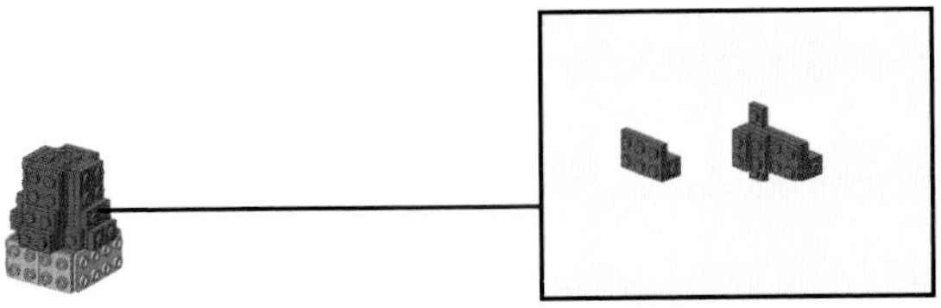

9

10

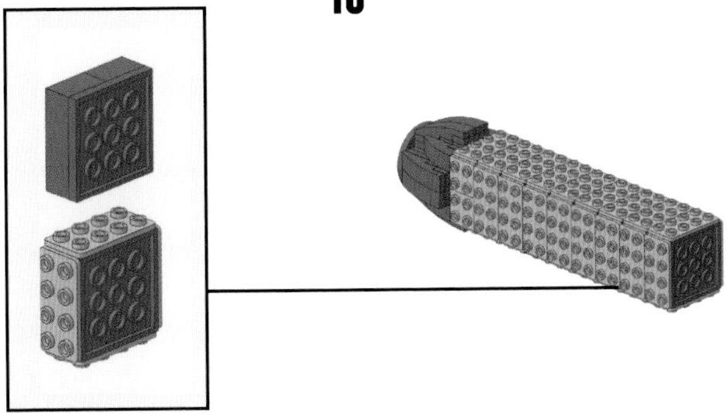

11

12

13

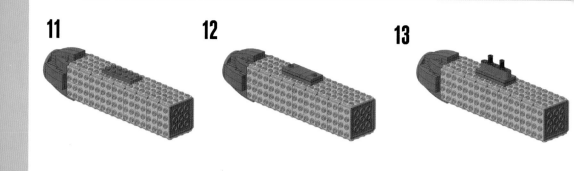

14

15

16

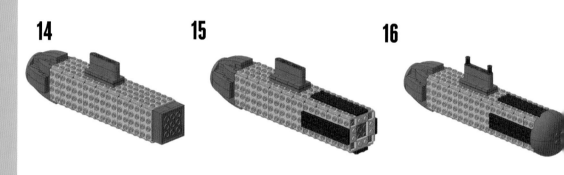

17

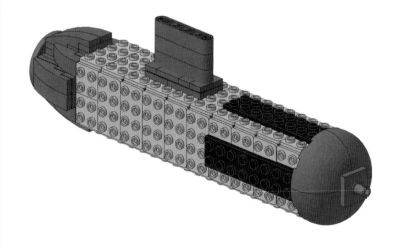

18

19

20

21

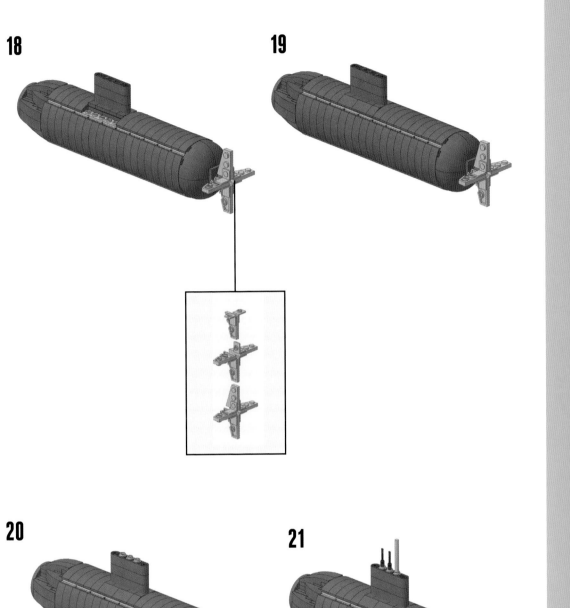

PASSENGER AND CAR FERRY

If it's not practical or cost-effective to build a bridge, a ferry is the way to regularly transport people and vehicles from one place to another. Ferries operate worldwide and vary widely in size, from those capable of transporting just a few people up to a Superferry that can transport hundreds of cars and thousands of passengers. There are many types of ferry, often designed specifically for the passengers that they carry and the ports they service.

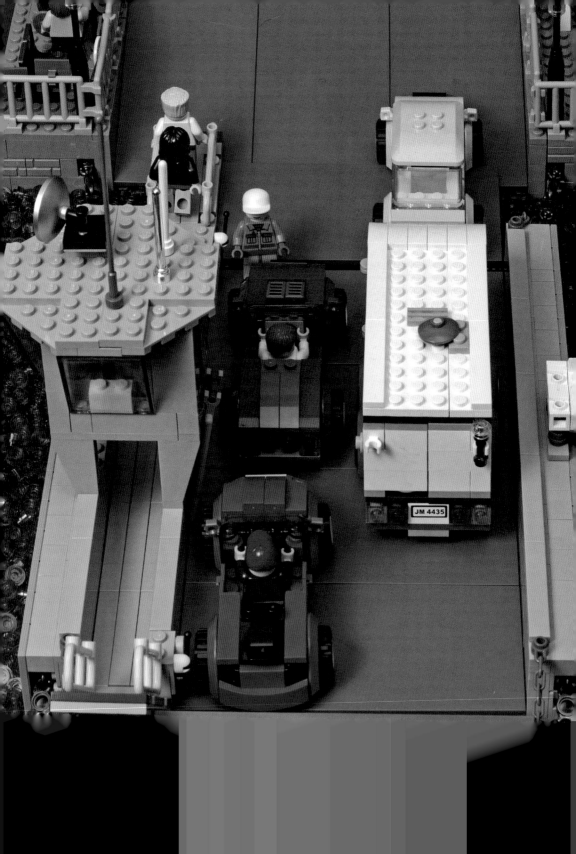

ferries with built-in ramps such as this one are sometimes referred to as ROROs (roll-on, roll-off), whereas larger
go ships are referred to as LOLOs (lift-on, lift-off) because they are loaded up with the help of an on-board crane. A
rid of the two is known as a ROLO. Now, if a RORO is large enough to contain accommodation for passengers it is
erred to as a ROPAX, and finally, if a RORO carries freight in containers as well as passengers and cars, it is referred to
a CONRO. Got all that?

WATER-SKI BOAT

If traveling inside a boat isn't your thing, how about being towed behind? That's what this boat is for. Its large engine is designed to pull a waterskier fast enough to allow them to travel on top of the water. Adult waterskiers might need to be traveling at 36 mph (58 kph) before they are able to comfortably ski! In fact, it's possible to water ski without the skis—although the boat needs to be capable of even higher speeds to overcome the extra friction.

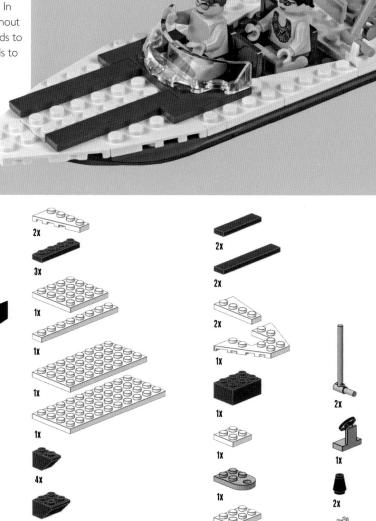

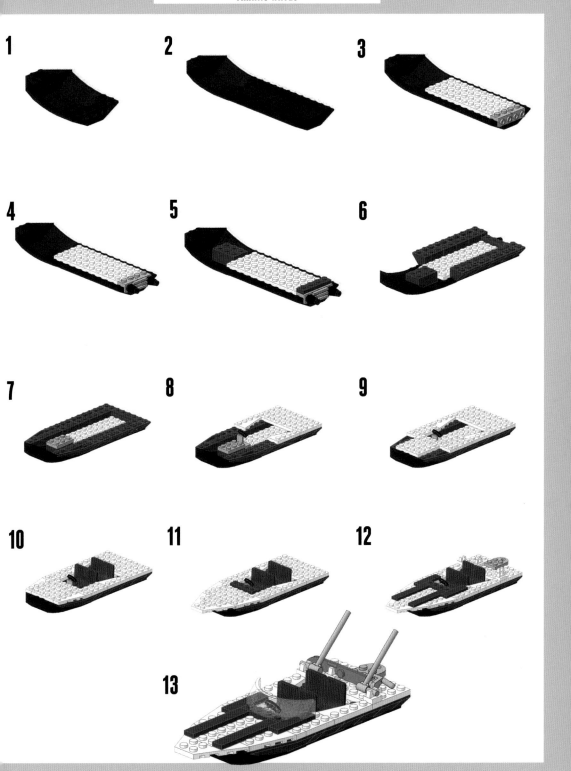

1

2

3

4

5

6

7

8

9

10

11

12

13

UNDERWATER RESEARCH VESSEL

If you need to inspect something deep underwater, sending down a diver can be complicated, dangerous, and expensive. Enter the ROV, or the remotely operated underwater vehicle. The ROV is a small submarine that is controlled by a pilot on the surface. It's much simpler to send an unmanned vessel deep underwater, and with the manipulating arms, lights, and cameras that many ROVs come with, they can carry out a wide range of tasks too.

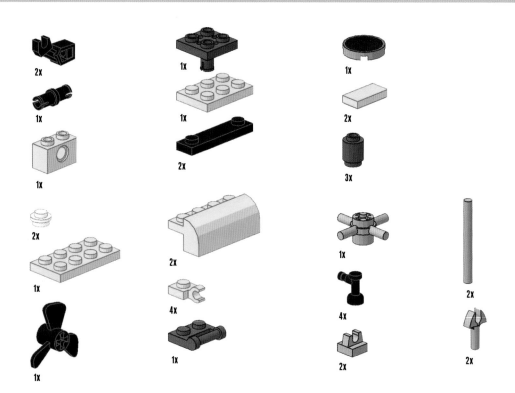

1

2

3

4

5

6

7

8

9

10

11

12

ZWARTE ZEE TUGBOAT

1962, Rotterdam, Netherlands

"Zwarte Zee" means "Black Sea" in Dutch, and this beautifully elegant ship from the Dutch company Smit International is in fact a tugboat. Commissioned in 1962, at the time the Zwarte Zee was the most powerful tugboat in the world. She had 9,000 horsepower at her disposal and could reach a speed of 16 knots/18 mph (29 kph) when she needed to. Sadly, after 20 years of service she was taken off the seas in 1984.

ugboats help tow or push other boats or waterborne vessels that are unable to move by themselves. Originally powered
y steam, they now run on diesel and are extremely powerful, although they vary in size depending on the body of water
ey are operating in. They are often fitted out with emergency rescue and icebreaking equipment. They even provide
ntertainment—tugboat races are popular events all over the United States.

CATAMARAN

Most ships only have a single hull, but those with two hulls are called catamarans. Using two slim hulls instead of one wide hull means that less of the ship is in contact with the water, reducing friction and increasing speed. This sailing catamaran is typical of a sailing "cat," with a lightweight mesh strung between the two hulls. Boats like this are often raced, and it's common to see one of the two hulls completely out of the water as it leans over against the wind.

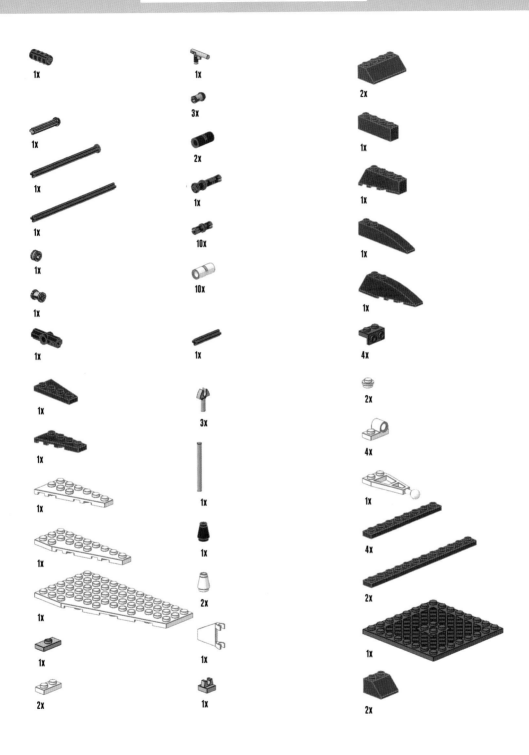

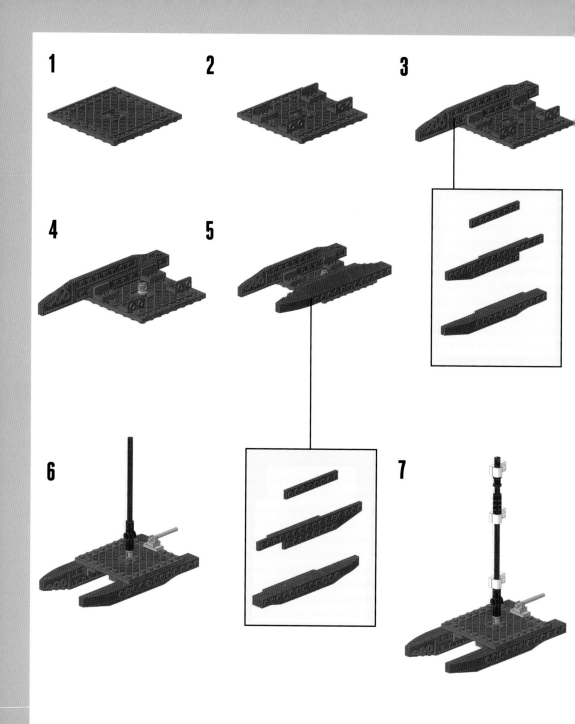

8

9

10

11

12

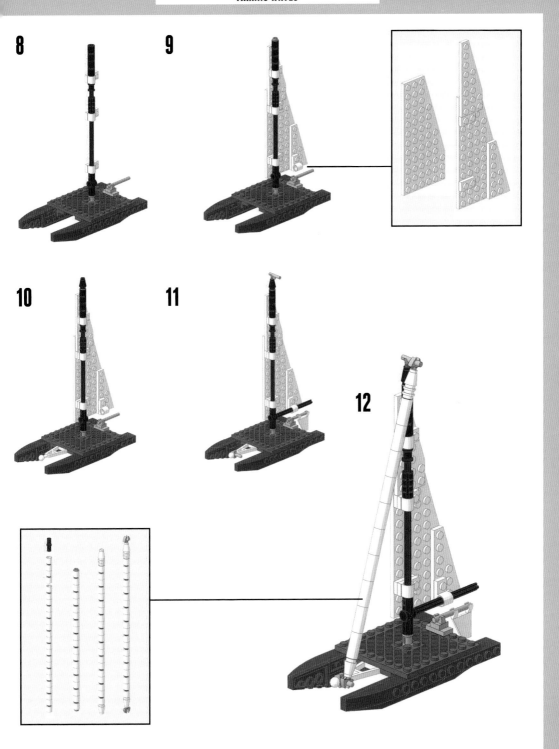

COAST GUARD PATROL BOAT

If you get into trouble on the seas, then these are the guys you call! This Coast Guard Defender is a model of the U.S. Coast Guard patrol boats. This type of craft is called "RIB," which stands for Rigid Inflatable Boat. The inflatable orange hull gives the boats a huge amount of buoyancy, which is good if you are trying to rescue people. The last thing that you would want to do when saving capsized boats is to capsize yourself!

RIB·24

PLEASURE BOAT

What better way to spend a sunny
afternoon than on the water?
This LEGO® pleasure boat would
be a great way to relax! Building
a boat out of LEGO is actually
more tricky than it looks. There are
certain special boat hull pieces, but
if you don't use one of those then
creating a smooth hull shape is quite
challenging. The builder of this boat
has achieved this by using curved
slopes, mounted sideways so that
they curve inward instead of down.

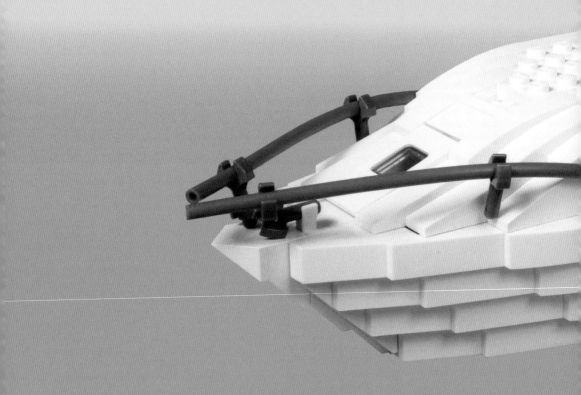

MONTGOLFIER HOT AIR BALLOON
1783, Ardèche, France

The French Montgolfier brothers invented this balloon in 1783. This was the first manned flight—ever. The balloon was made of taffeta, which was covered with a special fireproof coating. While they later carried out many flights with human passengers, it was wisely decided that the very first flights should have some "test subjects." The test subjects that they chose were a sheep (to approximate a person), a duck (that could fly anyway so should be fine), and a rooster (a bird that wouldn't normally fly to those heights).

HOT AIR BALLOON BASKET

What better way to see the safari plains than from a hot air balloon? Real hot air balloons float because the hot air inside weighs less than that on the outside. Our LEGO® balloon weighs 5½ lb (2.5 kg), though, so there's no danger of this one flying away with the passengers.

12x   2x

60x   8x   1x   4x   2x   1x

1

2

3

4

5

6

7

8

9

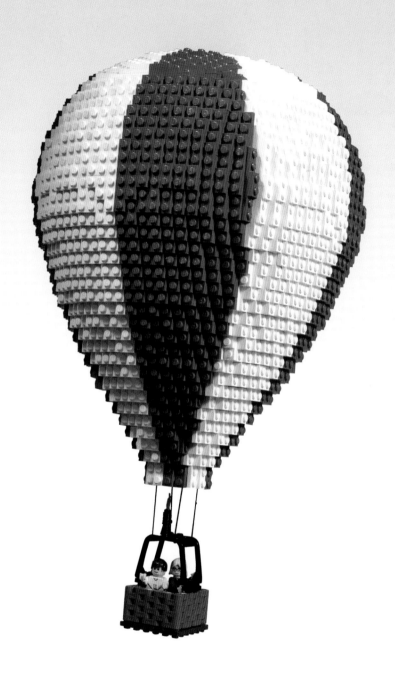

DA VINCI'S FLYING MACHINE

c.1480, Florence, Italy

Leonardo Da Vinci was a famous painter, but he was also a very accomplished scientist. One of the things that particularly interested him was flight. He came up with many designs for machines that could fly, including this one—an early design for a helicopter. His idea was for a rotating screw that would pull the vehicle into the air. Sadly, this could never have worked in his time—the technology simply didn't exist. However, this doesn't take away from the vision that he had more than 400 years before the Wright Brothers.

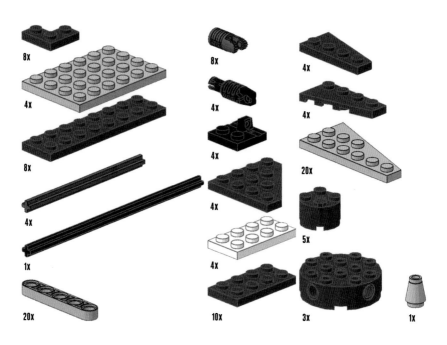

8x

4x

8x

4x

1x

20x

8x

4x

4x

4x

4x

10x

4x

4x

20x

5x

3x

1x

1

2

3

4

5

6

7

8

9

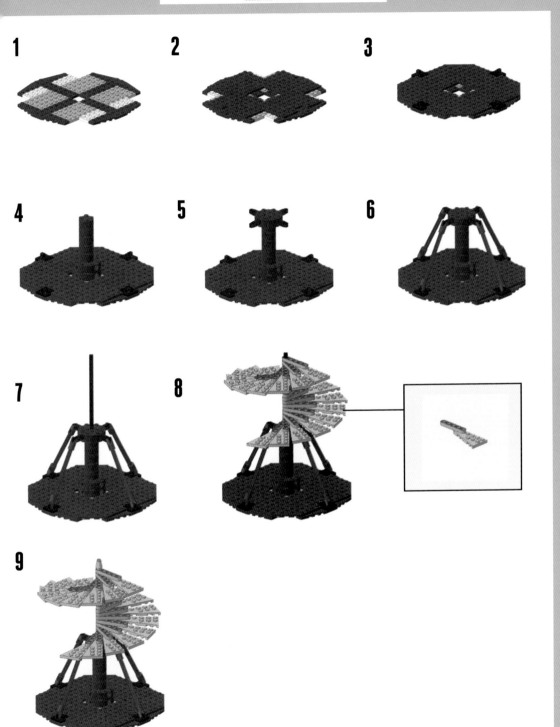

GOODYEAR® BLIMP

Did you know that there's a difference between a Goodyear® Blimp (like this one) and a dirigible (like the ill-fated Hindenburg airship)? Our blimp floats because it is filled with helium gas, which is lighter than air. It's also the helium gas that gives the blimp its shape—it's inflated like a giant balloon. Dirigibles, on the other hand, have a solid internal structure that keeps them in shape. Their gas is contained in giant balloons inside the ship. This blimp is modeled on a famous one that you might have seen at a football game.

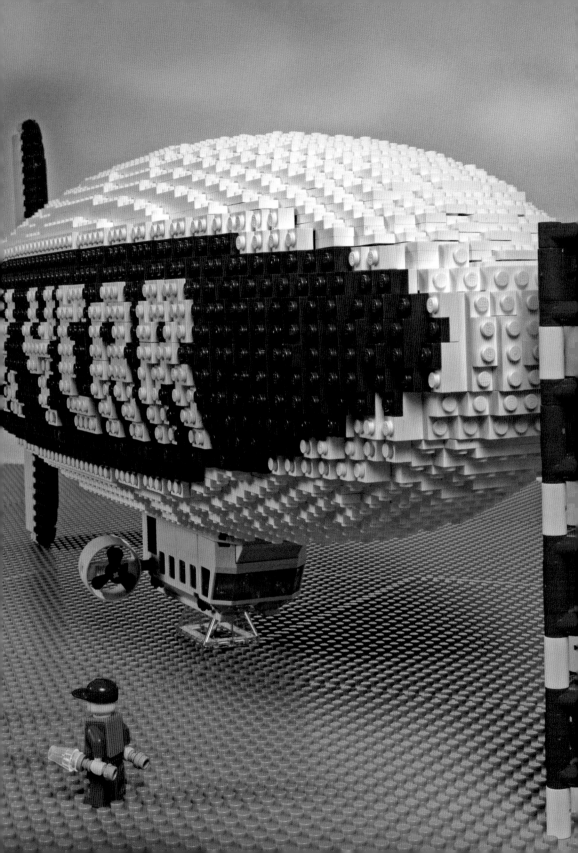

The original Goodyear® Blimp was developed by the Goodyear Tire & Rubber Company, which was founded in 1898 during the Industrial Revolution. Their first blimp was built at the oldest airship base in the United States, near Akron, Ohio. Goodyear's first airship was built in 1912, and the model evolved throughout the twentieth century, when it served a variety of purposes, including surveillance, aerial television coverage, and transmitting signals during rescue operations.

PARACHUTE

Should you suddenly develop a problem in the air, a parachute is what you'd be reaching out for. This one is designed for a different purpose, though—fun! Parachutes are made of a special nylon fabric, and such a thin structure is very difficult to model accurately in LEGO®. Instead, we've created a special design in the form of the Union Flag—the flag of the United Kingdom. You might recognize this from the 2012 Olympics, when James Bond and Queen Elizabeth II took the quick route to the games.

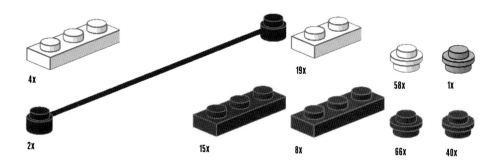

4x

2x

19x

15x

8x

58x

1x

66x

40x

1

2

3

4

5

6

7

8

9

10

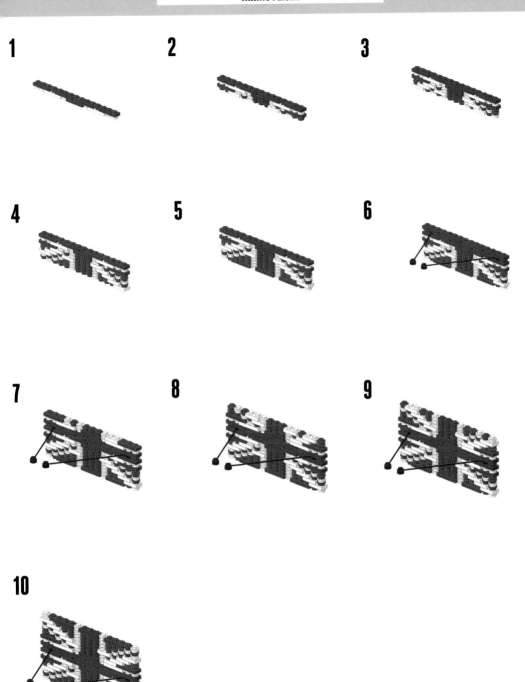

HELICOPTER

Helicopters are some of the most versatile aircrafts around. They can fly in any direction and hover in the same place. This makes them ideal for rescue services, such as the helicopter shown here. They produce their lift by rapidly rotating the blades above them. Each of the blades has the same cross section as an aircraft wing, so moving these through the air quickly generates lift. It takes a lot of effort to produce that lift though. Spinning the rotor blades at up to 400 revolutions per minute uses a lot of fuel, so helicopters have a limited amount of time that they can spend in the air.

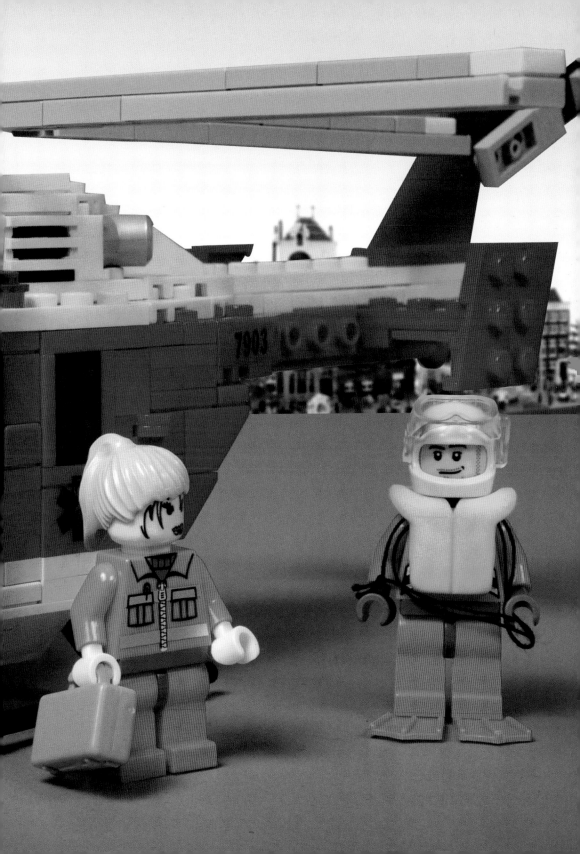

METEOROLOGICAL BALLOON

If you want to measure what's happening in the atmosphere, then the easiest way is of course to go there! Yet traveling up into the high atmosphere is a dangerous and expensive process. Much cheaper than using a rocket is to send some sensors up with a meteorological balloon. This model is based on one launched at the Halley Research Station in Antarctica as part of ongoing research by the British Antarctic Survey.

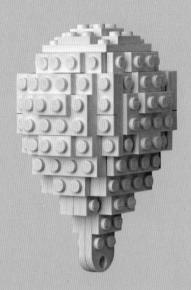

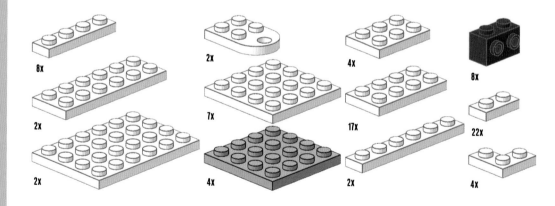

8x

2x

2x

2x

7x

4x

4x

17x

2x

8x

22x

4x

1

2

3

4

5

6

7

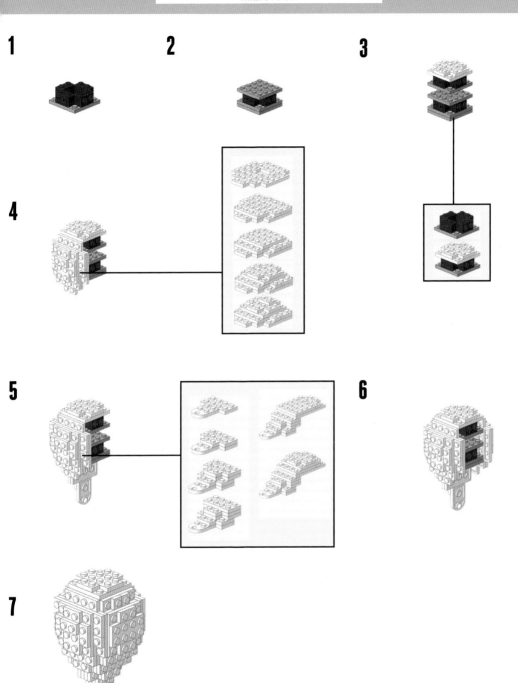

ese balloons are filled with hydrogen that is lighter than air and are then released to float upwards. Though they look all at ground level, as they fly higher and the atmospheric pressure reduces, they expand a great deal. These balloons n reach up to 25 miles (40 km) high before the pressure drops so much that the balloon expands too much and pops.

CONCORDE

1976, England and France

This plane is unique—it's the fastest passenger jet in history. The Concorde was built in a joint venture between British and French companies in the 1960s. It flew almost continuously until the year 2000. Its special wing design and engines allowed it to travel at a speed of Mach 2.02, more than twice the speed of sound, at 1,497 mph (2,497 kph). At that rate it could famously fly between London and New York in three and a half hours, and because New York time is five hours behind London time, you could theoretically land in New York before you took off.

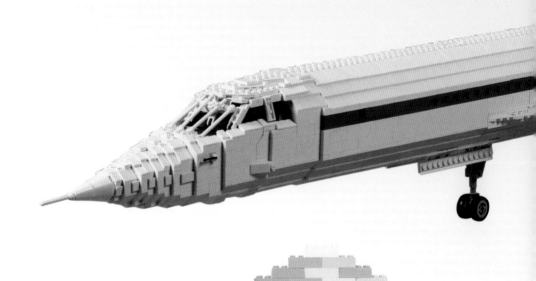

Hang Glider

Hang gliders have no engines—they simply (but slowly) fall to earth! With a hang glider, the pilot is suspended underneath a large wing with a rigid structure. Moving their weight from side to side lets the pilot control the direction in which he or she travels. As the hang glider is always falling through the air, pilots often launch from high ridges or hills and look for "thermals." A thermal is a rising column of hot air caused by the sun heating the ground. If a hang glider can successfully find a thermal, then he or she can soar upwards to extend their flight.

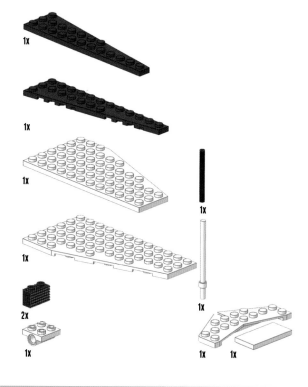

1

2

3

4

5

6

7

8

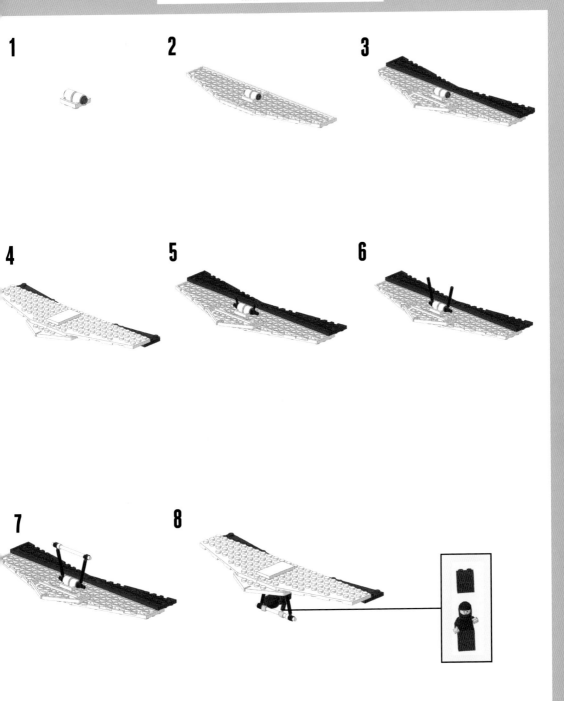

AIRPORT

No matter what type of air travel you are undertaking, there's one thing they all have in common. Airplanes require an airport. This one is based on a small urban airport, such as London City. Squeezed into a small dockland space, it must have all the same facilities as a much larger, international airport. Security is just as tight for the passengers, and there is a full fire crew on standby—just in case. The question is, where will our minifigures go on their vacations?

addition to passenger facilities and space for planes to come and go, airports also store large fuel tanks. Petroleum-used aviation fuel is stored where refueling vehicles are readily available to fill engines as required. Large airplanes use proximately a gallon (4 liters) of fuel every second, most of which is used during take off. Airports like this one also ed secure car parking facilities for those wishing to leave their cars over long periods of time. Happy travels, minifigs!

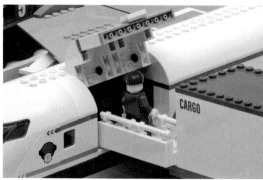

CESSNA 172 SKYHAWK

1956, Kansas, U.S.A.

Probably the best-known manufacturer of light aircraft is Cessna. This United States company has produced thousands of aircraft, but this is surely the most iconic—the Cessna 172. If you recognize this aircraft, there's a reason—it's the most widely produced aircraft in history, with more than 60,000 of these having taken to the skies. A Cessna 172 also holds the world record for the longest ever flight at a staggering 64 days.

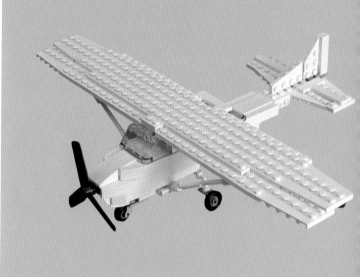

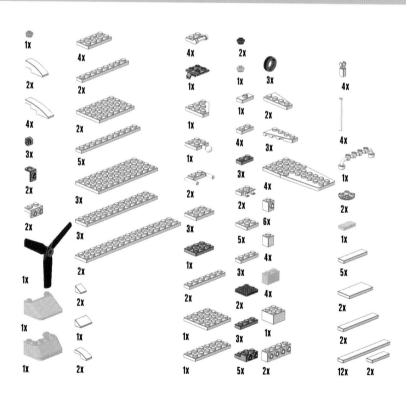

1

2

3

4

5

6

7

8

9

10
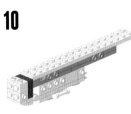

11

12
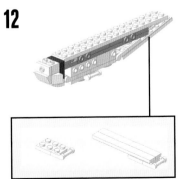

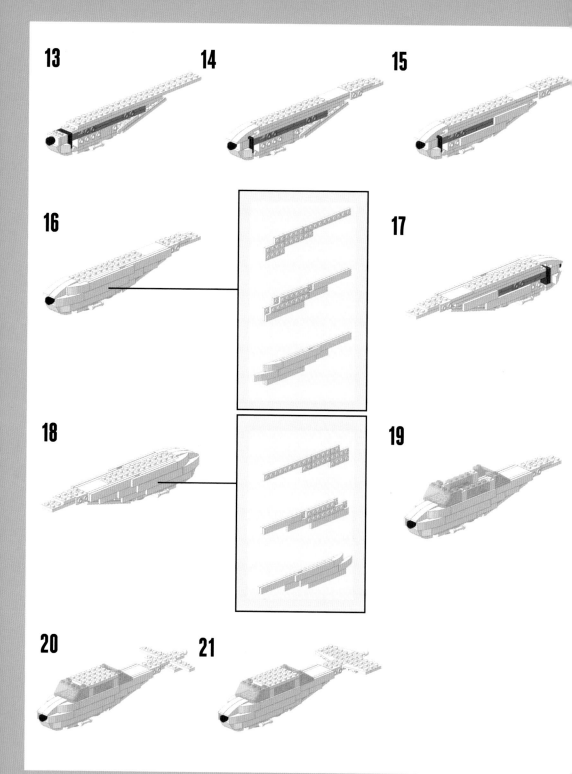

13

14

15

16

17

18

19

20

21

22

23

24

25

26

27

28

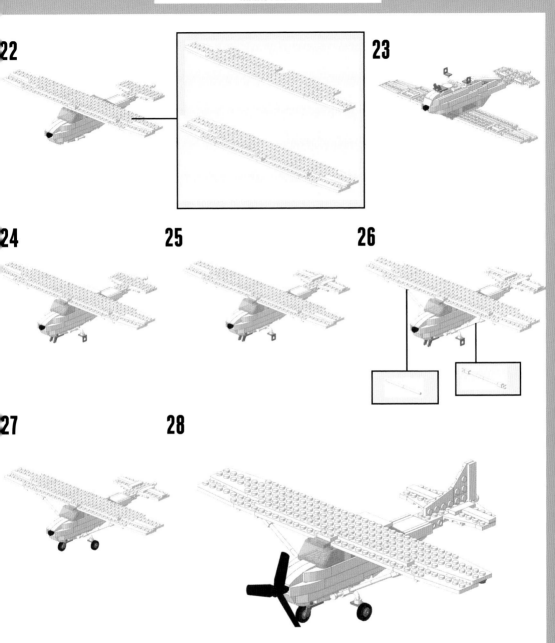

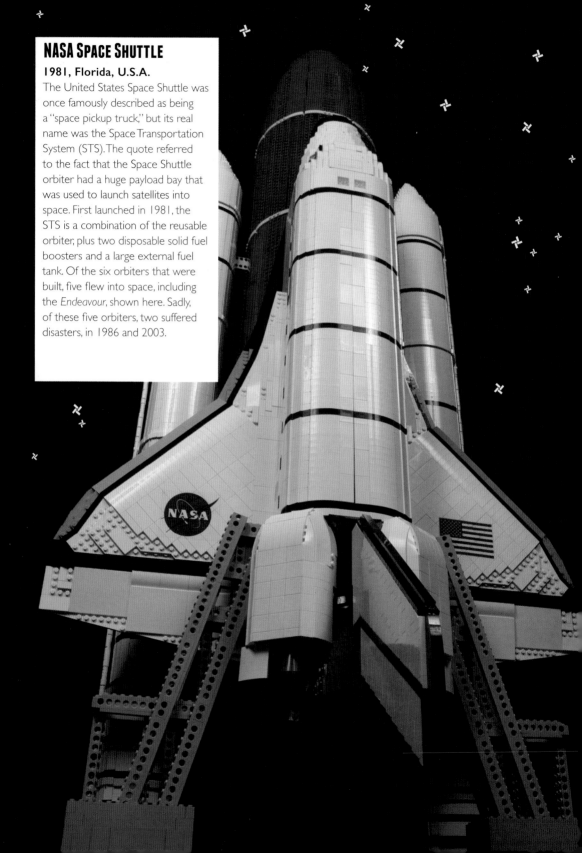

NASA SPACE SHUTTLE

1981, Florida, U.S.A.

The United States Space Shuttle was once famously described as being a "space pickup truck," but its real name was the Space Transportation System (STS). The quote referred to the fact that the Space Shuttle orbiter had a huge payload bay that was used to launch satellites into space. First launched in 1981, the STS is a combination of the reusable orbiter, plus two disposable solid fuel boosters and a large external fuel tank. Of the six orbiters that were built, five flew into space, including the *Endeavour*, shown here. Sadly, of these five orbiters, two suffered disasters, in 1986 and 2003.

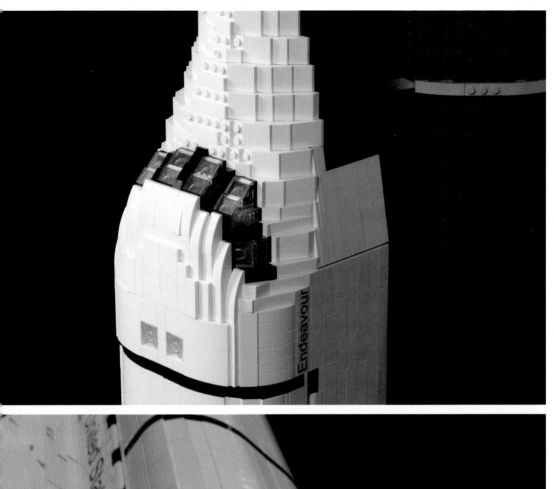

APOLLO LUNAR MODULE

1969–1972, Florida, U.S.A.

This is the Apollo Lunar Module (LM), the only vehicle to successfully be transported to the moon and take off again. Six lunar modules were landed on the moon by the United States between 1969 and 1972, and the lower halves of all of these are still there. The upper part of the LM is where the astronauts were housed, and when it was time to leave the moon, it blasted away from the lower half into lunar orbit. Sadly, this ascent stage had a short lifecycle. As soon as it docked with the orbiting Command/Service Module (CSM), the astronauts transferred into the CSM and sent the LM on its way—either to crash into the moon or into solar orbit.

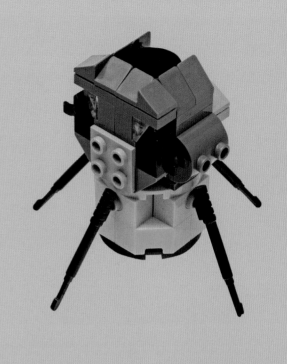

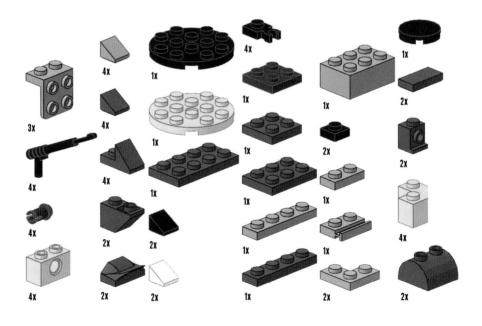

1

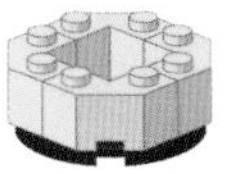

2

3

4

5

6

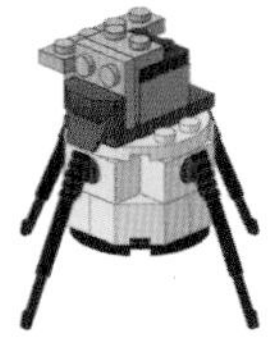

7

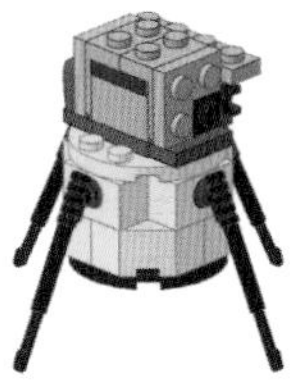

8

9

10

11

12

13

14

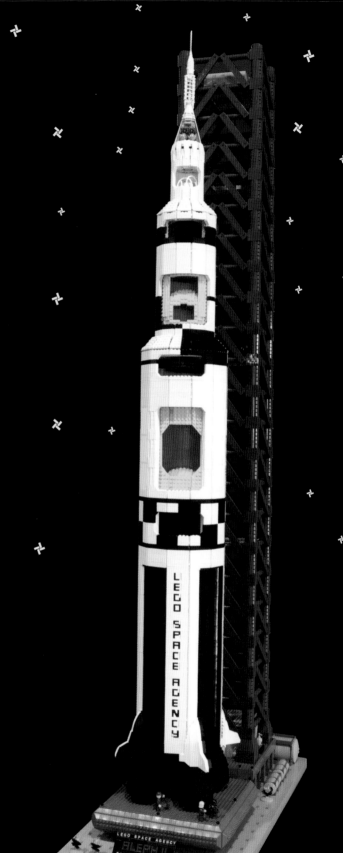

NASA Rocket

1966–1973, Florida, U.S.A.

This model is based on NASA's
Saturn V, which launched astronauts
into outer space on lunar missions as
part of the Apollo program during
the 1960s and 1970s. The rocket also
launched the Skylab space station
into Earth's orbit.

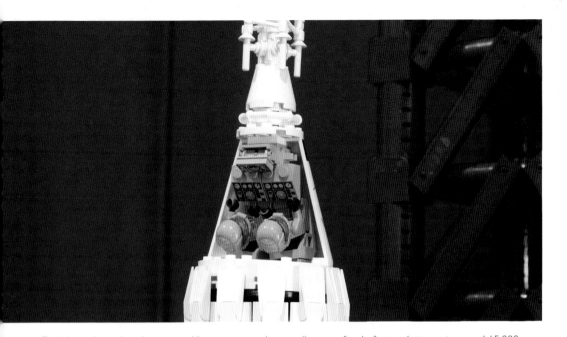

escape Earth's gravity and explore space, it's necessary to be traveling very fast. In fact, rockets must exceed 15,000 ph (24,140 kph) to make it into space. Moving large amounts of equipment into space requires massive amounts of rce, and the Saturn V was a three-stage liquid-fueled rocket. It burned a mixture of kerosene and liquefied oxygen that counted for most of the internal volume. Once the fuel in each stage was used up, the stage was dumped. This meant at there was less weight to propel forward and thus a greater speed could be achieved.

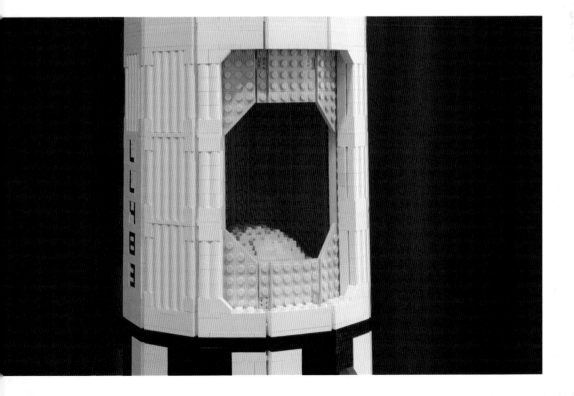

SPACESHIPONE

2004, California, U.S.A.

SpaceShipOne has a special place in aerospace history. It was the first privately funded manned spaceship. In 2004, SpaceShipOne took astronaut Brian Binnie up to an altitude of 367,454 ft (112,000 m) and into the edge of space. SpaceShipOne is almost unique in that it doesn't fly into space entirely under its own power. A companion aircraft, White Knight One, is used to carry SpaceShipOne part of the way. The spaceship is then detached and fires its own rocket to accelerate up to Mach 3, which is 2,284 mph (3,675 kph), and into space. This vehicle is leading the way for the commercial space flights of the future.

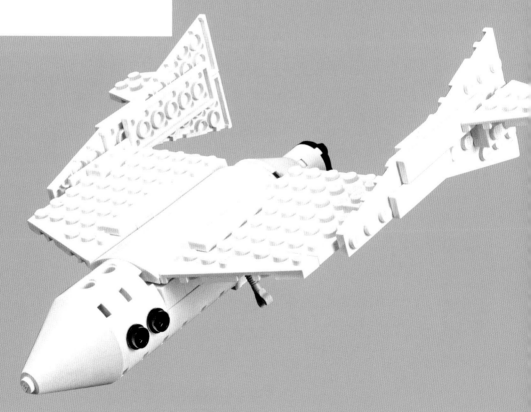

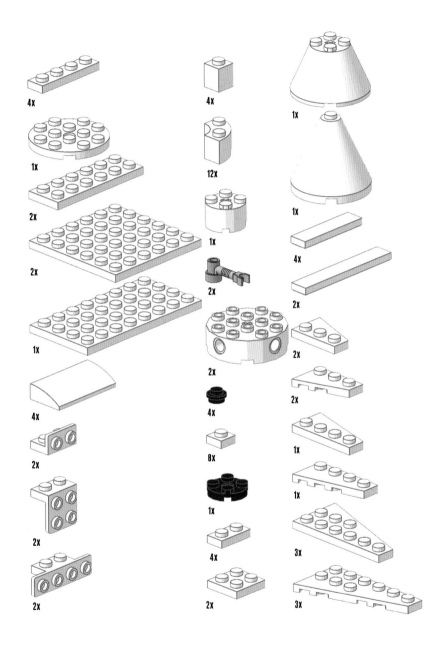

4x

1x

2x

2x

1x

4x

2x

2x

2x

4x

12x

1x

2x

2x

4x

8x

1x

4x

2x

1x

1x

1x

4x

2x

2x

2x

1x

1x

3x

3x

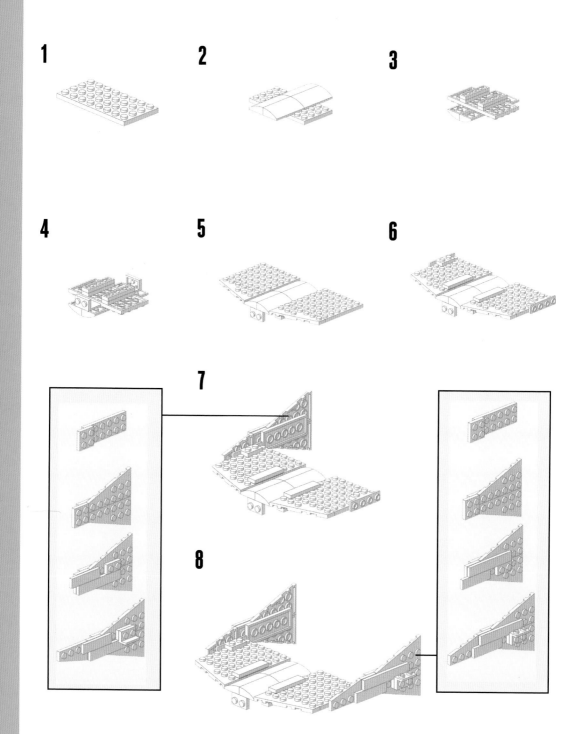

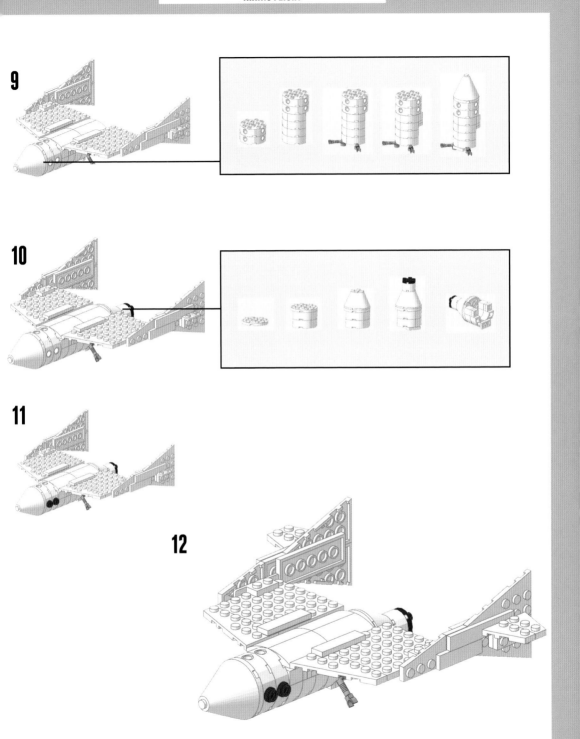

9

10

11

12

TIME MACHINE

There's one direction in which we've still yet to take flight—through time! Time travel has been a mainstay of science fiction since the genre was invented, and this time machine is one of the most famous. Taken from the 1960 film *The Time Machine*, based on a book written by H. G. Wells, this fantastical craft is designed to transport the passenger to any point in time—future or past. So, where would you go given the chance? Back to the log raft, the earliest water vehicle? Off to the Roman chariot races? Perhaps you'd like to see Stephenson's Rocket wow the crowds, or go forward in time to take a day trip to outer space? The only limit is your imagination!

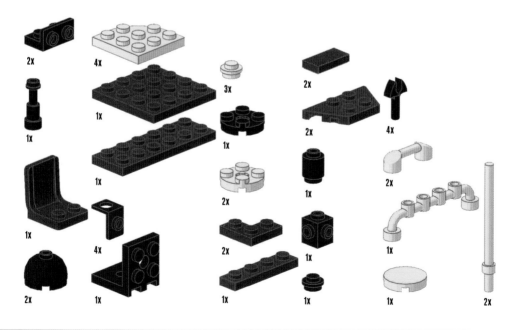

1

2

3

4

5

6

7

8

9

10

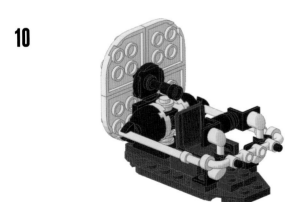

INDEX

BUILDERS AND CREDITS

Peter Blackert is an Australian AFOL, known as "LEGO911" online. His prodigious output of cars, trucks, and planes is well known worldwide, and he built the Formula 1 Racing Car on page 108.

Stuart Crawshaw started building with LEGO® bricks over 40 years ago, and is now a systems engineer living in Hampshire, U.K., with his partner Naomi Farr. Stuart built the NASA Space Shuttle (page 242) and NASA Rocket (page 246).

Adrian Croshaw is a LEGO fan from Bristol, U.K, whose iconic Seaside Tram features on page 146. He is an active volunteer at the Crich Tramway museum in Derbyshire, and it was this work that inspired him to build a LEGO tram.

Ed Diment is director of the professional LEGO building company Bright Bricks. He is well known for his huge model of the warship HMS Hood, the aircraft carrier USS Intrepid, and the airplane Concorde (page 228).

Kim Ebsen is an AFOL from Jutland in Denmark. He is a specialist hydraulic engineer, so he has a good insight into combine harvesters (page 44). Each of his large models takes around a year to create.

Warren Elsmore is an artist in LEGO bricks based in Edinburgh, U.K. He has loved LEGO since the age of four and is now heavily involved in the LEGO fan community. After a successful IT career he decided to work full time to help companies realize their LEGO dreams. Warren's first three books (*Brick City*, *Brick Wonders*, and *Brick Flicks*) were received to worldwide critical acclaim, and his models have toured museums and galleries across the U.K. For more information visit warrenelsmore.com.

Naomi Farr studied math at Trinity College, Cambridge, U.K. Now a member of the Brickish Association, Naomi has displayed her work in the U.K. and Europe, including the Penny Farthing (page 48), Hovercraft (page 182), NASA Space Shuttle (page 242), and NASA Rocket (page 246).

Carl Greatrix is a British AFOL based in Stafford, U.K. He was a vehicle caricaturist and cartoonist before working for TT Games. Now a Senior LEGO Model Designer, he also creates his own models, such as the Freight and Eurostar™ trains featured here (pages 150 and 164).

Klaas Meijard and Rene Hoffmeister are professional LEGO builders who travel all over the world to build. Together they created the amazing Cruise Ship on page 168.

Arjan Oude Kotte is a Dutch LEGO fan who builds minifigure scale LEGO ships for large companies. His Fishing Trawler features on page 176 and Zwarte Zee Tugboat on page 198.

Ralph Savelsberg is a Dutch physicist for the Ministry of Defence in the Netherlands who regularly writes for the popular LEGO blog Brothers Brick and is well known for his detailed scale models of aircraft. This book features his famous Fire Engine (page 62), Double-decker Bus (page 72), School Bus (page 84), Citroën 2CV (page 96), MINI Cooper (page 100), Digger (page 102), and Helicopter (page 222).

David Tabner is an AFOL based on the south coast of England and one of the founding members of the local LEGO train club there, as is evidenced by his amazing London Underground train recreation on page 134.

Ronald Vallenduuk is a Dutch LEGO fan, now based in Ireland, where his large-scale steam trains (page 124) are often exhibited in complete layout.

IMAGE CREDITS

All photography by Michael Wolchover and Warren Elsmore, with the exception of the following:

Alamy Chris Willson 26 (top)
Gareth Butterworth 22–23
Lars Jockumsen 168–171
Minifigs.me 26 (bottom)
David Phillips 21
Shutterstock 11, 20
Morgan Spence 27–29
Ronald Vallenduuk 124